# The Art of Doubles

## Winning Tennis Strategies & Drills

### SECOND EDITION

Pat Blaskower

**BETTERWAY BOOKS**
Cincinnati, Ohio

Other fine Betterway Books are available from your local bookstore or at www.fwbookstore.com.

21  20  19  18  17        14  13  12  11  10

Distributed in Canada by Fraser Direct, 100 Armstrong Avenue, Georgetown, ON, Canada  L7G 5S4, Tel: (905) 877-4411. Distributed in the U.K. and Europe by David & Charles, Brunel House, Newton Abbot, Devon, TQ12 4PU, England, Tel: (+44) 1626 323200, Fax: (+44) 1626 323319, E-mail: postmaster@davidandcharles.co.uk. Distributed in Australia by Capricorn Link, P.O. Box 704, Windsor, NSW 2756 Australia, Tel: (02) 4577-3555.

Library of Congress Cataloging-in-Publication Data
Blaskower, Pat, 1945-
 The art of doubles : winning tennis strategies & drills / by Pat Blaskower. -- 2nd ed.
    p. cm.
 Includes index.
 ISBN-13: 978-1-55870-823-5 (pbk. : alk. paper)
 ISBN-10:  1-55870-823-5
 1. Tennis--Doubles. I. Title.

 GV1002.8.B57 2007
 796.342'28--dc22
                                   2007006430
Edited by Michelle Ehrhard
Designed by Eric West
Illustrations by Eric West
Cartoons by Douglas Redfern
Production coordinated by Mark Griffin

## ABOUT THE AUTHOR

Pat Blaskower began playing tennis at the age of three, becoming a local junior champion at the age of twelve. In her career as a senior player, she has focused on the game of doubles. Before injuries forced her to retire from competition in 1995, she was ranked number one in the nation in Women's 35 Doubles, and number one in Northern California in Women's Open Doubles and Women's 40 Doubles. From 1985 to 1999, she coached league teams in Marin County and was the head tennis professional at the Mill Valley Tennis Club.

In 1999, she moved to Connecticut where, for eight years, every league team she has coached has reached districts, sectionals, or nationals.

Pat, also the author of *Women's Winning Doubles,* has a degree in English literature from the University of California, Berkeley. In the spring of 2007, she returned to California.

## DEDICATION

This is for my students,
You have taught me well.
It's been a great ride.
Thanks for the memories.

## ACKNOWLEDGMENTS

I have been overwhelmed by the enormous success of *The Art of Doubles.* Since its publication, I have learned much and revised my thinking in various areas of strategy and court position. I am proud to say that in my thirty years as a teacher and coach my league teams have reached districts, sectionals, or nationals consistently. But thirty years is enough. I will be retiring from teaching and coaching next year. This book is the sum and substance of all I know about teaching, coaching, and playing doubles. I am grateful to my editor, Michelle Ehrhard, for encouraging me to revise *The Art of Doubles.* It is a fitting end to this career.

# TABLE OF CONTENTS

Introduction                                           1

........... **Creating and Nurturing a Balanced Doubles Team**    6

**1**      *The Dream Team • Who Plays Which Court? • Nurture
           Team Character • The Dump • Do You Need a Coach?*

........... **Keep Your Team's Communication Lines Open**    17

**2**      *Communication Begins Off-Court*

........... **Learn Proper Court Position**    28

**3**      *What Exactly is Proper Court Position? • The Offensive
           Court Position • The Defensive Court Position*

........... **Win With Intelligent Shot Selection**    45

**4**      *Percentage Tennis • The Beginning Stage • The Middle
           Stage • Aim for the Right Targets • Other Targets to Aim
           For • Poaching the Ball • Closing the Net • Making Low-
           Percentage Tennis Pay Off • Know When to Bail Out of a
           Shot • The Shots You Need • The Shots You Don't Need*

........... **Develop Superior Poaching Skills**    67

**5**      *Plan to Poach • Reasons to Abort a Poach • Strategies for
           Poaching • Where to Hit a Poach • How Your Partner
           Figures into a Poach • To Signal or Not to Signal*

........... **Keeping Control of the Net**    84

**6**      *Handling the Dreaded Service Return Lob • Defending
           Against Lobs Other Than Service Returns*

**7** ............ Understanding Your Jobs on the Court      98

*Consider Yourself "On the Job" • The Server • The Server's Partner • The Reciever • The Reciever's Partner*

**8** ............ Flexibility: A Powerful Weapon      114

*Flexibility Requires Confidence • Ask Yourself a Couple • Key Questions • Recognize Your Own Predictable Strokes • The Australian Serving Formation • The "I" Formation Defending Against the Australian Formation • Defending Against the "I" Formation • How to Defend Against a Monster Serve • An Effective Tactic Against Impenetrable Opponenets • Flexibility in the Face of Lob Queens • In the End, Be a Gracious Loser*

**9** ............ Gaining Command of the Intangibles      129

*Time: There Never Seems to Be Enough • When to Use Depth, Pace or Finesse • Cultivate the Drop or Underspin Volley • Anticipation Means No More Scrambling • Two Rules of Proper Court Movement • The Gift of Great Hands • The Sum of the Parts*

**10** ............ Achieving Mental Toughness      145

*The Angst and Agony of Choking • Conquering the Two Greatest Fears on Court • Conquer the Fear of Winning • The Zone • Remember These Final Wisdoms*

**11** ............ Let's Talk About Winning and Losing      160

*The Ten Most Common Reasons Doubles Teams Lose Matches • The Three Keys to Winning.*

............ **Choosing the Better Arena to Showcase Your Team's Skills** 170

12    *League Tennis • Tournament Tennis*

............ **Drills for Honing Your Skills** 176

13    *Emotional, Technical, and Balance, Communication, and Mental Toughness • Proper Court Position, and Net Control • Intelligent Shot Selection • Superior Poaching Skills • Jobs on the Court • Flexibiliy • Command of the Intangibles and Timing Space • Charting Progress*

............ **Drills for the Highest Levels of Competition** 198

14    *Match and Clock Management • Groundhog Day Drills • Why Did You Lose that Game? • The Momentum Chart • Who Are Those Guys? • Looking for Tells*

# INTRODUCTION

Why do some doubles teams look like wooden soldiers and others like a pair of dancers whose movements seem synchronized to the sound of music only they can hear? All that running around on the court—where are they going? How do they know where to be?

There are, essentially, three kinds of doubles teams: those who make things happen, those who watch what happens, and those who wonder what the hell happened. Did you ever play against a doubles team that didn't seem to be particularly flashy, whose stroke production seemed inferior to yours, who didn't serve any aces or make many winners, and yet when it was all over, hadn't allowed you to win very many points, particularly the last one? Doubles isn't about big forehands and aces and crowd-stunning winners. It is a subtle game of grace, ball placement, and movement, whose masters often make others feel foolish or simply tempt them to beat themselves.

Players who watch what happens come in many varieties. There's the "I don't need court position because I can make a hole in your navel!" species. Then there's the "Come to the net all you want, sucker, because I'll just lob you and watch you chase it" tribe. And finally, with patience to match the sunny disposition the tribe is noted for, there are the players who will just get every ball back into play. They wait, contentedly, for you to finally lose patience and control and hit the fence with your easy putaway, and they watch, panting and smiling with victory, as you explode your two-hundred-dollar graphite racket into the net post.

Players who wonder what the hell happened also come in several varieties, none of which is famous for tactical or strategic prowess. Some are devout baseliners, committed to the theory that doubles is just like singles without as much court to cover. Others distrust the mystery of doubles and tend to disparage those things that they do not understand and are not curious or courageous enough to learn. These are the players whom you have heard say,

"I can't think and play at the same time. I just hit the ball." Freely translated, this means, "You can fill your head with fancy strategy all you want, but if I hit the ball hard enough at you, you'll probably miss, so why do I need all those expensive strategy lessons?" These players seldom recognize or acknowledge superior skills across the net, generally chalking up their losses to the windy conditions on their side of the net, the shadows across the court, poor lighting, tamale pie for lunch, a new, too old or not-broken-in racquet, or the always useful pulled muscle.

The what-the-hell-happened players provide the naiveté of the doubles world, and it is to these species that I attribute what are probably the ten most misguided statements about doubles play.

1. The player whose forehand is in the center always takes the center ball.
2. When my partner is serving, he takes the lob over my head, and I cross but remain at the net.
3. I never poach at the net because I'll get in my partner's way. Better to let him take the ball.
4. I never come to the net on my second serve.
5. There is no point to serve-and-volley tennis because you jus get lobbed all the time.
6. I like to play the deuce court because my forehand is so good (right-handed misguided statement).
7. When my partner is pulled wide, I must follow him, maintaining our No More Than Ten Feet Apart Axiom.
8. I like to hit deep service returns.
9. The best way to win a point at the net is to hit right at an opponent.
10. If our team is getting lobbed, I just stay back and leave my partner at the net.

Neither category of doubles team, not those who watch what happens nor those who wonder what the hell happened, possesses sufficient weapons to bother the highly skilled team, whose superior court position and shot

*The Art of Doubles*

selection combine to dispatch the pretenders-to-the-doubles-throne rather quickly. However, young and inexperienced teams are often very frustrated in their attempts to beat players whose skill levels, court position, and tactics they recognize as inferior to their own. This disparity between the longed-for success in the future and the short-term bitter setback is a prime reason rising young teams become disillusioned and ultimately abandon the quest. As a coach, I send uninitiated and eager teams out to play matches every day, only to have them return with their tails between their legs because they were crucified by the dreaded "lob queens." It is vital for players who aspire to be great doubles specialists to understand that it takes time to build the expertise and teamwork necessary for success. It takes far longer to develop a great volley, a penetrating overhead, good anticipation, and a feel for your partner's court position and shot selection than it does to learn to hit a decent lob and a good drive from the baseline. If you and your partner commit the time necessary to become an accomplished team, you will discover that by making things happen, you can continue to improve as long as you play the game and that the "watchers" and "wonderers" are forever stuck with a deck of cards that has no aces.

There are elements in common to all teams that truly make things happen to their advantage on the tennis court. Time and again, it becomes apparent that all great doubles teams appear to do the same things in very similar ways. It is not easy to quantify artistry, but that particular combination of elements inherent in the performances of distinguished doubles teams has the power to dispatch both the "watchers" and "wonderers" without missing a step and to create marvelous theater for the spectator.

Often these players do not possess superior stroke production. A one-hundred-mile-per-hour serve is not a strict requirement for an effective doubles player. The ability to bounce an overhead over the back fence is not essential. Further, this book enumerates the technical skills you need to achieve mastery and lists those that you don't need at all. Mastering the skills of doubles play is primarily about court position and graceful movement and the intelligent understanding of those intangible factors that may not be obvious from the sidelines, but which combine to keep a great doubles team's winning percentage consistently high. It is about these twelve elements displayed in common by all successful doubles partnerships:

Emotional and technical balance

Communication

1. Proper court position
2. Intelligent shot selection
3. Superior poaching skills
4. Control of the net
5. Understanding the different jobs on the court
6. Flexibility
7. Command of the intangibles
8. Mental toughness
9. Knowledge of what it takes to win and what causes teams to lose
10. Choosing the appropriate venue to showcase the team's talents

# The Key

Throughout this book, there are diagrams that help demonstrate the important points made and the skills that need to be learned. In order to understand how the diagrams are labeled, the below key has been provided.

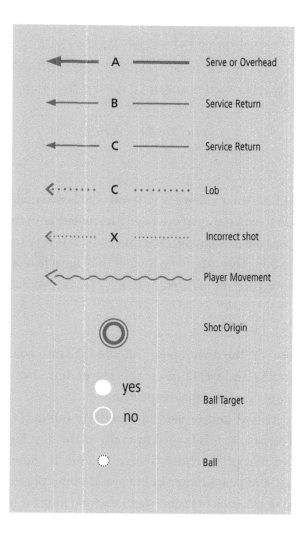

# 1

# Creating and Nurturing a Balanced Doubles Team

..............................

*Imagination reveals itself in the
balance or reconciliation of opposite or discordant
qualities; of sameness, with difference.*

..............................

*Samuel Taylor Coleridge*

Picking the right person to share your tennis life is no small matter. If you have aspirations to win national doubles titles, whether in the U.S. Open or as a forty-five year old in a seniors championship, it is very serious business indeed. Even if your goals extend no further than local league play, the decision should be weighed more carefully than, "Hey, you wanna play?"

## THE DREAM TEAM

Your own version of "the dream team" should take into consideration not only your strengths and weaknesses as a player, but also your ability to complement a potential partner's expertise.

When Billy Talbert and Bruce Old wrote *The Game of Doubles in Tennis* (published in 1956, it is regarded by many as the best book on doubles strategy ever written), they chose George M. Lott, Jr., John E. Bromwich, J. Donald Budge, and Jack Kramer as the best doubles players in the world and proceeded to ask each of them what he would look for in a perfect tennis partner. Their answers are as relevant to the game today as they were more than fifty years ago:

*To choose the perfect, or dream doubles player, there are, of course, many things to look for. However, after giving it much thought, these are the requirements that I would prefer. It goes without saying that this player must possess all of the basic shots, and perhaps excel in a few. He would forget all about trying to serve aces except for rare occasions, and concentrate on getting his first serve in as consistently as possible. He would at all times play his volleys deep and down the middle, using the alleys only when they were wide open, but even then hating himself whilst doing so. (However, the time deep volleys wouldn't be logical would be if the four players were in at the net; then a short or low shot at the opponent's feet is the answer ...) He should be able to play defensively as well as offensively. And he should have the type of personality that encourages talk during a match: there is nothing worse to me than having a doubles partner that won't "talk it up." There are always times when things aren't going well in almost any match, and if you can talk about these with your partner in an honest way, you can usually circumvent them.*
—**J. Donald Budge**

*As a first court doubles player [Mr. Bromwich is referring to the deuce court], I feel that to achieve success it is most essential for the player to understand the value of service returns which he must make with regular consistency. Returning-of-service is so important, and ability to appreciate the strength of your opponents against varying returns is essential. The player in the first court should endeavor to win the first point of each service, enabling his partner to try to force home the advantage and thus effect a breakthrough. He should be content to work for openings, be consistent with this return and prepared to forsake spectacular play in the best interests of developing teamwork and understanding with his partner.*
—**John E. Bromwich**

*In commenting on the qualifications for the ideal doubles player, I would like to emphasize a factor which is all too often overlooked. ... I want to stress antici-pation. ... The thing that separates the great from the near-great doubles play-ers is the uncanny ability to anticipate the actions of their opponents. There are four parts to anticipation ... placing your own shot and knowing what to look for ... learning the give-away motions of stroke production ... concentrat-ing on the motions of the opponent as he is in the act of striking the ball ... you and your partner shifting positions to meet the by-now well-anticipated return. Yes sir, give me a partner with the "feel" of anticipation and he will have made a long stride toward being the dream doubles player.*

—**Jack Kramer**

*As we know, doubles is mainly a matter of getting a service break, and then hanging on for dear life. Therefore, it behooves us to devise ways and means to obtain that service break. One way, of course, is through sheer power, but so few of us are able to do that that it is necessary to rely on cunning and clever-ness. I suggest that, like a baseball pitcher who throws his fastball, curve, and change-of-pace ball all with the same motion, the doubles player learn to make a forehand drive, a lob, and a soft, tantalizing shot ...with the same motion.*

—**George M. Lott, Jr.**

Not one of these experts is seeking the spotlight-grabbing power hitter who likes to hit through his opponents' navels. Each stresses intelligence, pa-tience, communication, teamwork, and artistic shot selection—skills that anyone with a commitment to becoming a winner can acquire.

## Winners Hate Losing; Losers Hate Winning

*A winner makes commitments. A loser makes promises. A winner says, "I'm good, but not as good as I want to be." A loser says, "I'm not as bad as a lot of other people." A winner listens. A loser just waits until it's his turn to talk.*

—**Anonymous**

If it were really true that it's not whether you win or lose that matters, but only how kindly you play the game, then the rules of tennis would not have included keeping score. The game is, after all, a competition designed to produce a victor. When shopping for a partner, bear in mind that winners hate losing and losers can't stand winning. Losers will find a way to fail in every close match you play, filling the air with excuses for every missed shot along the way. We all choke points and make mistakes, but a real loser has an emotional investment in continued failure and fears being successful. Loss after loss becomes a very comfortable easy chair, and the possibility of a win disturbs the status quo. These are the players who say to their partners, "I'm so bad. I just can't hit a ball," or "Those guys across the net are just too good. Maybe we'll get a few points if they double fault." This kind of attitude is just too discouraging for a partner and not likely to change without some serious soul-searching. Better to make sure you pick a winner—preferably a tall, fast, and crafty winner.

## Scenario for a Winner

Once you've canvassed the field and have your eye on a few winners, look for someone in this group who complements you emotionally. If you tend to rush through matches, sometimes even holding your breath during points, don't pick someone who is in as mad a rush as you are. Your play will look like a fast-forward image. You will never gain balance as a team and will probably wear each other out before the first set is over. Choose someone whose internal clock runs a little more slowly than yours and who can get you to pause and take an occasional deep breath. Conversely, if you are a plodder who prefers to think slowly and carefully, pick someone who can rev your motor a little and help you turn up the tempo of a match.

Emotional balance may not seem so vital, but it is critical to the rhythm of your teamwork. During a match, the time you spend not hitting a ball—the between-points time—far exceeds the time you actually spend playing a point. What a team does during the between-points time will often determine whether it can maintain momentum within a match, and whether it can steal momentum from the opposition while they are napping. In addition, the team that manages this down time better, using it to change strategy, suggest a play, or give added encouragement to one another, will almost always be the victor in a tight match. If you and your partner have just lost a must service game, you have also lost momentum. A doubles team of two fast-forward types is not likely to slow down in the next game and is probably not capable of the careful execution needed to wrest momentum back. These are the players who will try to "hurry up to catch up" and will likely make far too many unforced errors. The match may slip through their hands while they are bustling around the court. On the other hand, two plodders are likely to brood and sulk over the lost service game, thereby elating the opposition by their sullen behavior to the point that momentum is so entirely in the opponents' hands that the match cannot be saved.

## WHO PLAYS WHICH COURT?

Having chosen a tall, fast, and smart winner who complements your emotional makeup, you must decide who should play which side of the court.

Most good doubles players serve down the middle at least 80 percent of the time. If both you and your partner are right-handed, consider putting the stronger backhand service return, and/or backhand volley, in the deuce (right) court and the stronger forehand service return, and/or forehand volley, in the ad (left) court. If your partner is a lefty, contemplate his effectiveness in the ad court. Most lefties have an uncanny ability to step around a serve and execute a topspin forehand that drops on an onrushing server's shoes at a viciously sharp, short angle. Lefties seem to do this naturally in a way most right-handers can never hope to duplicate. If your partner is a left-hander, you might want him in the ad court simply for this wicked service return.

On a right-handed team, the player in the ad court will take most of the overheads. Make sure that player is up to the task. If you have a lefty in the ad court for that devastating service return, the lob down the middle is a problem and requires some fancy footwork by both players to assure that the ball can be played as an overhead. If your lefty partner is in the deuce court and you, a right-hander, are in the ad court, it could be a racquet-clashing free-for-all on the lob unless your communication is superb.

Finally, every team should have a "setter" and a "hitter." Often, though this is not a hard-and-fast rule, the "setter," as alluded to by John Bromwich in his comments about the "first court player," plays the deuce court and should be both psychologically and technically suited to the role. This player should be content to set the point up and allow the ad court player to claim the glory. Steadiness and dependability, percentage tennis (see page 46 for a discussion of percentage tennis), and much "plain vanilla" should be this person's forte. The setter's skills should also allow extensive use of the offensive lob as service return (because the ball carries over the backhand of a right-hander's opponent and often produces a weak lob that can be handled as an overhead smash by a right-handed hitter positioned in the ad court).

The "hitter" should be the team member whose personality is more that of a risk-taker and whose technical skills include the ability to hit clean winners and low percentage returns of serve. This player is generally positioned in the ad court because the score is always uneven when he is returning serve. The ad court player receives serve at every "break point" (except the 15-40 point) and at the beginning of every service rotation in a tiebreak. At certain critical points in the match, he must have the courage to go for the winner rather than rely on his opponent to make an error.

Not all of the factors leading to court assignments will fall on the proper side of the issue. You may own a rapier backhand but be a "setter" at heart. You may have a great overhead but don't trust your right-handed forehand down the middle under pressure. Your partner may definitely be the "hitter" but is also wedded to the deuce court. Ultimately, you evaluate each of your strengths and arrange to display those while hiding your weaknesses as best you can. But regardless of the considerations, you both must return serve well. If you can't break serve, you can't beat anybody. While you're at it, it is an excellent idea to decide who should serve first for your team. Whoever serves first will be the player serving at the critical 4-5 or 5-4 juncture in the match. The decision should not just be based solely on who has the better serve. You want the first server to be the player who is more likely to have nerves of steel under the pressure of serving for the set or serving to stay in the set.

## NURTURE TEAM CHARACTER

Out of the balancing of sameness with difference comes the character of your team. Playing well *as a team* is the common goal, and each of you, while bringing unique contributions to the endeavor, is responsible for making sure that the confluence of skills results in a smoothly running machine. If your partner's lob volley is the envy of the circuit but you can't execute it, stop trying and keep enough balls in play to allow him to showcase it. If he gets anxious and worried when you're behind, develop the skills to keep his head in the match and learn to act confident and unconcerned. If he tends to become serious and withdrawn under pressure, balance it out. Take a class in stand-up comedy. Trust your partner and his judgment. Have pride in your team and learn to carry yourselves confidently on the court—shoulders back, racquets up. You win together and you lose together.

## THE DUMP

One of the most painful experiences in the life of a doubles player is the moment of the "dump." Whether you are the "dump-er" or the "dump-ee," it is not a pleasant experience and can seldom be managed without someone feeling rejected or ill-used.

*The Art of Doubles*

There are times and situations in a partnership when it is in both players' best interests to find new partners, and the split ends up mutually beneficial. And there are times when the "dump-er" perceives a real or imagined advantage to breaking off the partnership while the "dump-ee" would have been quite content with the status quo.

Sometimes it takes playing together for as long as a year before partners discover that they are simply incompatible and don't complement one another's talents. It may be as obvious as two personalities that don't mesh or as subtle as an inability to regulate the internal clock speed. If you play your matches at a speed of around eight and your partner likes to perform down around four, it may be that, instead of balancing one another, you make him rush his shorts and he makes you yawn. If so, your team cannot establish a comfortable playing rhythm.

Two players learn to play doubles together at a certain stage of their development. They take lessons together, practice together, and play tournaments together. Often one has the raw talent to blossom very quickly into a much more highly skilled player and does, and the other has less natural ability and learns far more slowly and so becomes "the weaker player." Sometimes the player lagging behind perceives the situation and sometimes he doesn't, but the rising star always is aware of the difference. This is the most difficult problem a doubles partnership will ever have to face. Often the advanced player hangs with the situation, says nothing, and ignores the problem, but the losses become frustrating and resentment can creep onto the court. Painful as it may be, the two players should frankly discuss and recognize the legitimate need for the budding star to move on.

Sometimes people's priorities change. A player may have been totally committed to the task of becoming a great doubles team only to find that he cannot spare his partner the practice time the team needs. Perhaps he finds that it is not activities unrelated to tennis that intrude, but rather his commitment to the game of singles. Single matches are almost always played before doubles matches, and a player who finds himself consistently involved in long, three-set singles duels will simply not have the energy to finish a grueling doubles match. In this case, the partnership should be amicably dissolved, and the doubles specialist should seek someone whose priorities are not so fragmented.

In some cases, the partnership may be functioning on the court as well as can be expected for the level of experience the team has gained, but one of the players will become impatient and dissatisfied with the win-loss record. This kind of player tends to be a great critic of his partner's weaknesses and a poor analyst of his own abilities. He fails to understand that a winning record must be amassed slowly, through time and trial and error, and is unaware that victory cannot be purchased. This player seems to have a new partner every week, constantly blaming each discard for every match lost. He seeks the proverbial Rosetta stone, convinced that success lies just around the corner if only he had the perfect partner. A player dumped by this kind of partner is well rid of him and should rejoice.

Whether it is a legitimate difference over practice methods or doubles philosophy, incompatible personalities, or an aversion to gum chewing, the decision to end the doubles relationship should be mutual.

## False Promises and the Dating Game
Some of the unpleasantness of the dump can be averted if you avoid several common traps. Beware of the overly eager beaver who will promise you anything just to claim you as his prize. This type of player is always on the lookout for someone who is much more skilled than he is. He wants to ride your coattails to victory and has no intention of putting in the time or work necessary to improve his game. When you win, he will take the credit, and when you lose, yes, it is your fault. He is blissfully ignorant of his own weaknesses and feels that the time *you* put in on the practice court should be enough for both of you.

Guard against those who like to play the dating game. These are the players who will be loyal to their partners only until someone they consider more skilled catches their eye. You may feel that after working together for two years, sharing victories, and practicing your skills, that you are building a solid on-court relationship. But the minute your partner spies a bigger serve or a more lethal forehand, he will dump you. He may cite "wanting to go in a different direction," or "needing a change of scenery," but in reality he has spotted a more intriguing prospect and will not hesitate to move beyond you.

When you commit your time and energy to learning the game of doubles with a partner, first and foremost, you have to really like that person. Second, you must trust that person. Third, you must respect that person. You will be in for as many rough days as splendid ones, as many failures as triumphs, as many disappointments as wonderful surprises, and how you treat each other under pressure will ultimately determine the health of your doubles partnership.

## DO YOU NEED A COACH?

You and your partner probably already take some lessons, but that isn't the same as hiring a coach. "What is essential is invisible to the eye," says Antoine de Saint-Exupéry's Little Prince. A good coach should possess the sensitivity of the Little Prince's friend, the fox, and the skin of an armadillo. If he does, he can be a valuable asset to your development as a skilled team. A good coach should not only conduct practices for you, but also attend your matches. What you and your partner *thought* you did in a particular match and what you *really* did on the court that day may be two different things. The coach should gently point out the ways in which you deviated from good court position, failed to take advantage of opportunities presented to you, or fell into bad habits. And he needs to be brutally but kindly honest with you. If you played poorly, you should be told. If you were brilliant, you should be lavishly praised.

Without an unbiased eye monitoring your play, you really don't have an objective evaluation of your performance. You may not even be able to assess why you won or lost. A good coach is an essential part of your repertoire and every aspiring doubles team needs one. Without an experienced adviser, you might be in danger of joining the "wonderer" clan—those who come off the court asking, "What the hell happened out there?"

## Balance Checklist

- ☐ Make sure you pick the right partner—one who complements you emotionally and technically.
- ☐ Consider carefully who should play the deuce court and who should play the ad court.
- ☐ Understand that teamwork means balance and that the goal is not to showcase one player, but rather to play well as a team.
- ☐ If your partnership just isn't working, dissolve it amicably.
- ☐ Watch out for false promises and those who play the dating game.
- ☐ Treat your partner with respect, and the team will develop self-esteem.
- ☐ Hire a good coach.

# 2

# Keep Your Team's Communication Lines Open

....................................

*A fool may talk, but a wise man speaks.*

....................................

*Ben Jonson*

You are serving at 4-5 in the third set of a vital tennis match. A win means your entire United States Tennis Association league team goes to a sectional competition. The score is 15-30. Your partner turns to you and says, "Come on, get this point. We need it!" That statement pushes your heart rate and blood pressure close to those of someone critically ill. Your anxiety level goes off the chart, and you're fortunate if your serve makes it to the net on three bounces. Your partner has made a common mistake. Rather than speak calmly and quietly about a plan for the point, the player succumbs to the pressure, abdicates all responsibility for this critical situation, and really says to the server, "*You* do it! Please, God, don't let the ball come to me!" This kind of communication is so destructive that it may lose the match.

## COMMUNICATION BEGINS OFF-COURT

Good communication between partners starts before you take the court and should include a brief discussion of the day's game plan, including strengths and weaknesses of opponents, if known. If your partner for the day isn't your regular partner, decide beforehand who will play which side of the court, who will serve first, and whether you will choose to serve or receive. Don't walk on the court and allow your opponents to witness a conversation such as this one:

"What side do you play?"
"Oh, I don't care. Do you?"
"No, not really. Shall I play forehand?"
"Okay. Shall we serve? We won the spin."
"Oh, I'm not very confident of my serve. You want to serve?"

After a discussion like this one, be assured that your opponents are, at best, supremely confident and, at worst, sure that you two are a couple of lunatics who quite possibly have no idea what you're doing.

All good doubles teams communicate frequently between points (sometimes after every point if it is a very critical game). They share ideas, give positive and specific suggestions for point playing, encourage one another to stay confident, and even sometimes confess to anxiety or "choking." This kind of dialogue is much easier when you are winning and much harder, although more crucial, when struggling to reverse a losing situation.

Dr. Allen Fox, sports psychologist and contributing editor to *Tennis Magazine*, commenting on the psychology of tennis, said, "Winning requires solutions, not descriptions of problems." The player who spends valuable between-point time lamenting to his partner, "This sucks. I can't return serve. They're too good," is certainly describing the problem, but he appears to be fresh out of solutions. How much more constructive if that player would say instead, "I'm having trouble with that big serve. I'm going to try a lob. Be alert."

Let's rejoin that anxious server, whose partner has just unwittingly rendered him nearly catatonic at 4-5, 15-30. How much more useful it would have been for his partner to say, "You serve down the middle, and I'll poach the return." Anytime a partner gives a suggestion for a particular serve or return or combination of shots, it alleviates some of the pressure and allows both players to share equally in the responsibility for the outcome of the point. Good doubles teams know this and experiment with solutions to problems. When things get rough, they never retreat into sulky silence, leaving their partners alone, exposed to the enemy, and fearful to utter even simple words of encouragement.

## Golden Rules of Good Communication

• **In general, always err on the side of speaking too much, not too little**. Great doubles teams don't make assumptions, and they don't leave things to chance. "Yours" or "Mine" should be uttered every time there is any question as to who will hit the shot. Thinking your partner is going to hit the ball, only to see it bounce unplayed on your side of the court is an example of assuming what should be carefully designated. Never stand idly by and watch your partner struggle to keep his eye on the ball and worry whether or not his feet are in the court and whether or not he might play an "out" ball. Always help with a clear and loud "Bounce it," if appropriate, or "Out!" if you believe it is going out. Never assume your partner can read your mind. If you intend to try a very wide serve on the next point, or a passing shot down the line, or if the score permits a low-percentage return, tell your partner your plan so that he can be ready before the opponent's play and not be surprised by it at the last minute.

• **Be aware of your body language**. Body language is probably the subtlest and most overlooked form of communication with your partner. Dr. Jim Loehr, author of *The Mental Game* and consultant to the USTA Junior Development Program, encourages players to "look on the outside the way you want your partner to feel on the inside." Nobody loses points on purpose, and if, when your partner blows the perfect setup into the bottom of the net, you are a shoulder-slumper or a sigher or a hands-on-hips starer, it won't be long before your partner decides that the rules have been changed to permit three against one.

- **Trust your partner and never undermine him.** If you believe he blew a call, don't indicate to your opponents that you're either playing with a cheater or a candidate for bifocals. Tell your partner quietly that you believe the call to be in error and let *him* correct the mistake, thus preserving the team unity in your opponents' eyes. If you're about to hit a ball and your partner tells you to let it go, do it. Don't hit the ball anyway and then tell your partner that you know better which balls are good and which will sail out. Trust on the court is a vital component of confidence.

- **Communication on the court must be a dialogue, not a state of the union address.** Many times one player will have no trouble being vocal while the other, perhaps shyer, partner is content to listen and say very little. Players must share the responsibility equally for keeping the communication lines open because certain situations demand assertiveness from even the most timid teammate. For instance, as the server's partner, you will help him greatly if you have the courage to tell him where you would like him to serve, suggest a kind of spin, call different team formations, or even predict that a lob is in the offing. Shrinking violets have trouble assuming this responsibility, and yet doing so allows the serving partner the luxury of sharing the burden for winning the service game.

- **Playing with a taciturn sphinx really complicates the need to communicate effectively.** As the crosscourt player you begin the point, either as the server or the receiver. Because you are coming off the baseline, you are behind your net player and are in a position to see the whole court better than your partner, who is hugging the net. Therefore, the crosscourt player is always team "captain" and is responsible not only for calling out the score when serving, but also for issuing all verbal commands to his partner. But many of my students just can't seem to talk to their partners during a point. As the cross-

*The Art of Doubles*

court player, they rely on the excuse that they simply can't talk and hit at the same time. But that excuse doesn't fly because your commands should come out of your mouth *before* you deal with hitting the ball. One member of a doubles team I know is so reluctant to speak on the court that she actually has her net player call the score when she is serving. Sphinxes often feel that any verbal communication will ruin their concentration and cause them to make unforced errors. They mistake silence for focus. And yet, when you are the crosscourt player, you simply must utter certain commands. This is not optional. Dealing with lobs is the crosscourt player's responsibility, and he is required to tell his partner whether he wants him to "stay," "switch," or "come back" (see chapter six). If he fails to direct his partner before dealing with the lob, then his poor net player will spend the point craning his neck to guess where he belongs on the court. Worse, if the crosscourt player fails to call him back, the net player may become the target for an opponent's overhead. At first, trying to master the flash cards "stay," "switch," and "come back" is difficult. Sphinxes often stand rooted to the court wearing blank stares as they try to determine quickly which direction to give to their partners. And they are always terrified of uttering the wrong command. Like all other facets of the game, practice is the cure. Sphinxes will never be chatterboxes on the court, and they usually would prefer to be left alone on the court in order to concentrate more effectively. They do not wish to be "chatted up" and encouraged. Regardless, crosscourt players—all sphinxes included—are responsible for the health and welfare of their partners who are hugging the net. Crosscourt players *must* learn to speak. They control the team's positioning and formation.

• **Both partners should communicate kindly, thoughtfully, positively, and confidently, even under the most adverse circumstances**. Each player must trust that his partner will be receptive to constructive criticism or suggestions for improving the team's performance, even though the chances for victory at a particular moment may be dismal. It is all too easy when things are going badly to become silent, withdrawn, and essentially resigned to the inevitable loss. At this point in a match, many players actually become afraid to say anything to their partners. The courage to "talk it up," as Don Budge puts it, must come from someone, so if it isn't forthcoming from your partner, then it must come from you.

• **Good communication built on trust serves to avoid the ethical problems that sometimes arise**. Many players state, unequivocally, that they will never overrule a partner's call. Regardless of whether this refusal is out of fear of reprisal from the partner, or simply loyalty, it is nothing less than cheating. This scenario is one familiar to all players:

You serve what you think is an ace. Both you and your partner think the serve was good, so one of you asks the opponent who called the ball out if he is sure. "Yes," he says. Then you turn to his partner and politely ask if he saw the ball. "No, I didn't see it at all," he says. Maybe he really didn't see the ball, but if that team is a never-overrule-your-partner team, you can rest assured that he will *never* have seen *any* ball his partner calls out. Adhere to the standards expressed in the USTA publication, *The Code*, which deftly handles all ethical problems on the court. Memorize the following lines of a great poem on tennis:

*Call questionable balls their way, not yours; you lose the point but have your concentration, the grail of self-respect. Wear white. Mind losing.*

From *Tennis* by Howard Wilcox

Your tennis reputation is a vital part of your on-court presence, and unpleasant as it may be, you must overrule your partner's call if you clearly see a ball differently. Start with the assumption that you are both honest players and that each of you trusts the other's judgment. Given that information, it is reasonable to assume that everybody blows a call now and then. If your partner feels that you called a ball incorrectly, he should immediately tell you, softly and privately, and you should make the correction to the opponents. The whole issue of line calls in tennis is such a charged one that players tend to overreact. If your team corrects a call that you have made in error, do not worry that your opponents will immediately brand you as cheaters. In fact, it is quite the opposite. By having the courage to reverse your own call, you will most certainly gain their respect.

- **Always present a united front**. Take the court together, sit together on the changeover, and leave the bench together after each rest period. Not only is this behavior important because it facilitates last-minute communication of ideas, but it also is designed to send important messages to your opponents.

Some opponents, whether deliberately or unwittingly, try to use the "divide and conquer" approach. Everyone knows that the time for polite chitchat is *after* the match, never before or during, and yet some opponents will try to isolate one of you and solicit your attention, breaking your concentration and your unity as a team. If you remain together, this tends not to happen, as they are loath to try to engage both of you. The minute one of you is sitting alone, you are subject to being taken under the wing of the enemy, thus leaving your poor partner the lone adversary.

My partner of several years ago (with whom I won a national doubles title) was a wonderfully tough competitor and also a kind, friendly, and warmhearted individual. On one occasion, we were playing a match in which we had quite a comfortable lead midway through the second set. At some point we lost a ball over a fence, and I offered to retrieve it. When I returned to the court several minutes later, I found my partner and both of our opponents sitting on the bench together avidly discussing their mutual preferences in tennis clothes, shoes, and racquets. When the match resumed, we quickly lost six straight games before we righted the ship, regained our concentration, and closed out the match.

While you can control interaction with your opponents during a match, sometimes avoiding prematch fraternization with the enemy is awkward. If you play league matches, you know that socializing is as much a part of the event as the competition, and it is very tough to maintain that balance between "putting on your game face" and being a gracious hostess to or guest of the other team. You and your partner must remember that the point of taking the court in the first place is to compete fairly but unmercifully, taking advantage of every miscue your opponents make. It becomes most difficult to maintain that attitude if you have just made, minutes before the match, two new lifelong friends out of your opponents. The strategy that seems to work best for my students in this predicament is to use platitudes. It is fine to comment on what a lovely day it is, but avoid mentioning that the heat could be a factor in the match. Be polite and gracious, but do not get into a long conversation with your opponent-to-be about how your strained shoulder is feeling or how powerful his new racquet has proven to be. Save substantive conversations for *after* the match.

In the environs of a sanctioned tournament, it is often easier to avoid prematch interaction with your opponent's because socializing is really the last thing on anyone's mind. Everyone has come to the event with the sole purpose of demolishing the opposition. Occasionally, however, unavoidable pitfalls arise.

In July of 1992, my partner and I played the USTA National Senior Women's Grass Court Championship in Haverford, Pennsylvania. The event is played, as long as the weather holds, on the most beautiful grass courts in the world. That year, a torrential thunderstorm descended upon us on the day of the semifinals, drenching the courts and, in the groundskeeper's words, "closing the grass" for the remainder of the tournament. Matches were completed not on *twenty-five* grass courts, but rather on *four* carpeted indoor courts. Obviously, scheduling became chaotic, and as many as one hundred players were crowded into a small viewing area awaiting their turn to play.

Avoiding our opponents became nearly impossible unless we chose to stroll through the deluge outside. One of the women we were scheduled to play cornered my partner and explained that these indoor courts were virtually her home turf. She bragged of her ability to hit every line on the court, indicated that she and her partner were the home-crowd favorites because they lived in the area, and questioned the expertise of two Californians not only on the now-soggy grass, but also on a carpet we had never set foot on. I was well aware of what was happening, but short of being rude to someone enjoying the support of the club members who were hosting this tournament, I could do nothing. I decided our psychological rebuttal would have to wait for the match.

When it was finally our turn to play, my partner took the court nervous and a little shaky. Our garrulous opponent was still at it, chattering away at my partner. I said nothing. In the first game of the match, on the first point our friend served to me, I hit a forehand service return between the two opponents for a winner. The next time she served to me, I was able to win the point with a volley I hit right at her navel (not generally my first choice of targets). At this point, I had silenced the biased crowd and muzzled our chatterer. My partner settled down and proceeded to play some of the best tennis of her career, earning applause and respect from the audience. We went on to win the match, but it was a struggle.

I believe we would have won the match in any case because we were the better team, but clearly the prematch interaction between our opponent and my partner (couched in the guise of polite conversation but obviously intended as psychological warfare) was an obstacle we would rather not have dealt with.

• **Get help on the court from the officials in charge when you need it.** Finally, in an unofficiated match, the most uncomfortable moment on the court comes when a team needs to call for a linesperson. This puts a tremendous strain not only on your communication with your partner, but also on your ability to communicate further with your opponents. If you feel that your opponents are repeatedly making incorrect line calls, you simply must stop the match and ask the tournament officials for help. Often one team member will feel that the situation warrants a linesperson but is loath to call for one for fear of upsetting either his partner or the opposition or both. A conversation between partners might sound like this:

*"That's the third time my ball has hit the back line and they've called it out."* (Translation: "Those guys are cheating, and I want to call for a linesperson.")

*"Hey, partner, just ignore it and aim a little shorter."* (Translation: "Don't you dare make waves. I don't want to be embarrassed and have people think we're bad sports. Our opponents would probably never speak to us again. They're very nice people and probably just need glasses.")

To avoid the embarrassment and the divisiveness of this situation, teammates should discuss their strategy for this eventuality before they ever begin the match. Both players need to understand that they have a right to expect proper line calls from their opponents, and if fairness is not forthcoming, the outcome of the match may be jeopardized unless they take steps to correct the situation. Calling for a linesperson can be done quietly and gracefully, and as simply as, "I think we need some help out here." Doing this does not label your team troublemakers or monsters. If it becomes necessary to ask for help, stand united as a team. Don't let one partner make the unpleasant declaration while the other runs to the net, wringing his hands and apologizing profusely to the opponents for the inconvenience.

Anytime you call a linesperson to your court, further necessary communication across the net becomes strained at best. A team must understand that this is a regrettable but unavoidable consequence of their actions. A tennis match is not a popularity contest, and the goal is not to endear yourselves to your opponents but rather to emerge victorious—fairly and honestly.

If, having requested the assistance of an impartial observer, you question the wisdom of your decision, evaluate the end result. If the questionable calls stopped after the arrival of the linesperson, then you halted deliberate cheating. If the same calls were made, only to be overruled by the linesperson, then your opponents were probably fair people in desperate need of an optometrist.

In all facets of life, the ability to communicate well is a learned skill, and it is always more difficult in a crisis. As with all dimensions of your tennis game and your teamwork, communication must be practiced to be effective. The results are well worth the effort.

## Communication Checklist

- ☐ Communicate well with your partner. This strategy often makes the difference between a win and a loss in a tight match.
- ☐ Issue the necessary commands to your partner.
- ☐ Battle the tendency to "shut down" emotionally when things are tight. Talk more, not less, under pressure.
- ☐ Never take the enemy under your wing, or vice versa.
- ☐ Don't be timid. Stand up for your rights—together, as a team.

# 3

# Learn Proper
# Court Position

....................................

*Reason, in itself confounded, saw division grow together.*

....................................

*William Shakespeare*

Court position is one of the few variables in this wonderfully maddening game that is entirely under your control as a player and as team. In any given match, you will have to deal with your opponents' winners (those superior shots you just can't get your racquet on), your own unforced errors (because everyone makes them), and those lucky mis-hits off your opponent's frame that I call "Oh wells." There is nothing to be done about these inevitabilities, but you can certainly put yourself in the right position to deal with whatever is hurled your way.

Many, many players are wedded to the notion that proper court position is wherever you happen to be at a particular moment. The "watcher" or the "wonderer" of the doubles court is frequently glued to the baseline, leaving his partner alone, unhappy, and far too vulnerable at the net. This "one up, one back" formation will prevail against inferior teams with poor volleying skills, but the gaping holes in the court created by this poor positioning will be quickly exploited by a good doubles team adhering to proper court position. In addition to all the other misery (bickering between partners and arguing about the center ball) this formation invites, it also leads inevitably to the need for the player on the baseline to lift every ball he hits for it to clear the net. Unless every shot he executes is a perfect lob to the edge of the baseline, the results will be decidedly ugly. The properly positioned net team will make things happen by hitting down on those high balls and aiming for the baseliner's exposed and quaking partner. Dirty looks and harsh words will undoubtedly follow.

## WHAT EXACTLY IS PROPER COURT POSITION?

"Court position" refers both to your distance from the net and to the distance between partners in any given situation. Technically, there are only two "positions" on the court, one offensive and one defensive. The goal is for both partners to achieve one of those positions simultaneously so that the entire court is well protected from penetration by your opponents' best shots. Both positions should reflect the symmetry and balance necessary to stave off any attempt by your opponents to confuse you, cause you to wonder which of you should take the ball, or find a hole in your formation. Attaining the offensive court position is the primary goal in every point. The defensive court position is one forced upon you by your opponents.

## THE OFFENSIVE COURT POSITION

There are as many theories about what constitutes proper offensive court position as there are tennis professionals teaching the game. I firmly believe in what can be referred to as the "staggered formation." Since I have been teaching this system, all of my league teams have reached districts, sectionals, or nationals. When I moved to Connecticut, my students started calling this theory "California Doubles." I find this an apt moniker because several California tennis professionals I respect, namely Helle Viragh and Henry Kamakana, teach this method of court positioning.

The theory I embrace relies upon a crosscourt player and what I call a "terminator," and it is based upon preventing the most devastating shot in doubles—the crosscourt lob. The problem with most conventional models of offensive court position is that they insist both players remain side by side and close the net together. If a savvy opponent executes a crosscourt lob against this formation, one of the players has to run faster than the ball is traveling to catch up to it because the angle of the ball is increasingly moving away from the team. This togetherness at the net has three other serious problems:

1. Which player should cover the lob? The faster player? (And do we run a quick race to determine this?)
2. Whose ball is the center ball? Does it belong to the forehand? What if your partner is a lefty? Does it belong to the player who hit the last ball? (And who is keeping track on his sleeve?)
3. Who puts the ball away? Both? (Somebody better duck.) The more aggressive player? (And what is the litmus test for that attribute?)

The staggered formation neatly solves all of these problems and also prevents the crosscourt lob. The crosscourt player never closes into the net (unless switching jobs with the terminator, as will be discussed later). His position varies from several feet inside the service line to a step or two behind the service line, depending on how likely it is that a lob is in the offing. Because all points begin crosscourt, the server and receiver begin all points as the crosscourt players. Their job is not to win the point, not to close the net, but to keep the ball crosscourt, stay patient, and set up their respective terminators for the point-ending volley. The server's partner and the receiver's partner are the terminators, so designated because the crosscourt player begins the point by placing the ball in front of the terminators, that is, *on their side of the court.* The serve will land in front of the server's partner, and the crosscourt return will land in front of the receiver's partner.

To reiterate, anytime the ball is on *your side of the court,* you are the terminator. Anytime you are *crosscourt from the ball,* you are the crosscourt player. Ideally, the terminator's goal is to attain a position about four feet from the net. If the service return is a deep lob over the server's partner, then the receiving team's jobs are reversed, and the receiver becomes the terminator by virtue of the fact that the ball is in front of him. Anytime the crosscourt player chooses to lob in a straight line, he has opted to make himself the terminator. This changes the job of the receiver's partner because the ball is now crosscourt from him. The lob option is a legitimate change of direction and does not violate the "deep to deep, short to short" rules discussed in chapter four. The crosscourt player must remain positioned at least eight feet behind the terminator. This distance reminds both players of their jobs. The crosscourt player is the "setter-upper" and "lob coverer." The terminator is just that—the one who takes *only* short lobs as overheads and finishes off points with punishing volleys. The jobs *do not overlap.*

The distance between the partners and angles they use to address the ball are just as important as the team's proximity to the net (see diagram one). The use of the center netstrap and the concept of the "mirror" are useful guides to the geometry of the court. Both partners should be very careful to position themselves in the middle of the probable angles of return. The crosscourt player should always use the center netstrap to angle himself directly crosscourt from the ball. If the ball lands in his crosscourt opponent's alley, he should slide toward *his own alley* until the center netstrap intersects the ball placement. If the ball lands in the middle of the crosscourt opponent's court, near the center service line, then the netstrap would bring him very close to that center line. Bear in mind that if you hit a wide volley or service return and move in the direction you have hit the ball, you are totally out of position—nearly the reverse of where you should be on the court.

While the crosscourt player works with the netstrap, the terminator uses the "mirror" concept, and the most important element of this visualization is that the mirror has a *convex corner on the outside.* The mirror is flat in the middle but has a rounded edge as the ball placement moves toward the alley. Near the center line, the terminator is positioned directly in front of the ball, but as shots are traded and the ball placement moves toward his alley, the player stops physically moving and begins a bow-like swivel to face the ball placement in the alley. *Under no circumstances should the terminator find himself standing in the alley opposite the ball.* He has opened up the entire middle of the court.

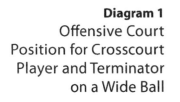

**Diagram 1**
## Offensive Court Position for Crosscourt Player and Terminator on a Wide Ball

The crosscourt player uses the netstrap while the terminator uses the convex mirror to remain in the middle of the probable angles of return. Despite the actual distance between the players, the middle is not open.

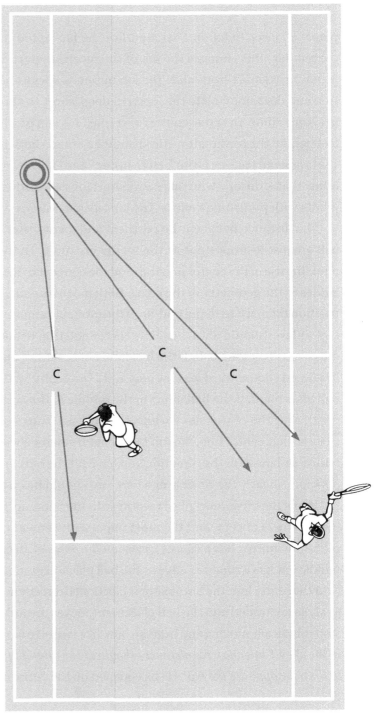

*The Art of Doubles*

Diagrams one and two show the correct and *incorrect* positions for the crosscourt player and the terminator as the result of an extremely wide volley or service return played to the opponent's alley.

When I place a ball in the alley on my teaching court like the one in the diagram and then place my students in the correct positions, they look at one another in horror and turn to me aghast that there is so much space between them on the court. But as long as both players are facing the ball, with their feet angled properly, the court is not open because both players are in the middle of the probable angles of return. The idea that players should always move together on the court, or the "windshield wipers" theory, is a myth, and it doesn't work because it exposes all the angles on the court. Similarly, when I place a ball very near the center service line and guide my students into the correct positions (see diagrams three and four for correct and *incorrect* positioning), I see the "You've lost your mind, coach," look in their eyes. And yet, so long as your team keeps your balls low, your opponents have no angles from the middle of the court, so again, the netstrap and the mirror have the court covered.

Earlier, three important questions were posed. Who covers the lob? Who covers the center ball? Who puts the ball away? The answers now seem obvious:

1. The crosscourt player covers the lob.

2. The center ball first belongs to the terminator if he can hit down on it, or to the crosscourt player who is positioned to execute the shot by using the netstrap.

3. The terminator always puts the ball away.

I once gave this demonstration to an inexperienced league team whose members were delighted with the ways in which they could anticipate the flight of the ball. When I asked for questions, one aspiring star said, "Gee, this is great, but would it work in a match?" Yes, it does work in a match, to the point where your opponents can't figure out how you can be in so many places at once.

The entire offensive line adjusts slightly forward or back, depending on the likelihood of the lob. If the opposition is that misguided "one up,

## Diagram 2
## Improper Positioning on a Wide Ball Exposes the Middle

The crosscourt player has not aligned himself with the netstrap and the terminator has moved too far into his alley, thus exposing the middle of the court and the angle.

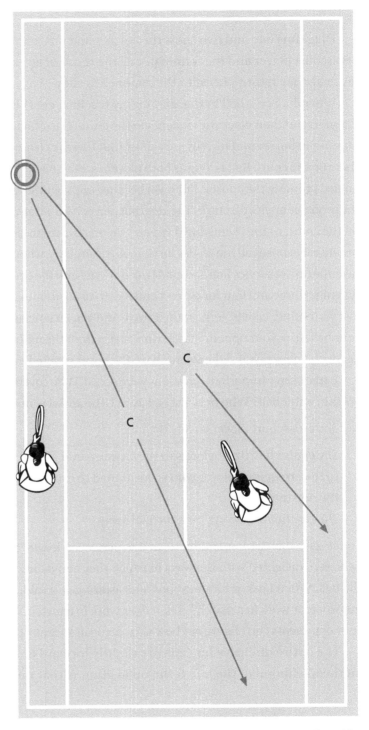

*The Art of Doubles*

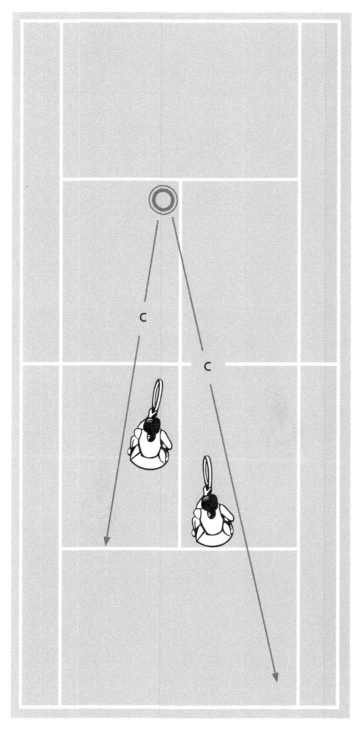

## Diagram 3
## Offensive Court Position for Crosscourt Player and Terminator on a Middle Ball

The crosscourt player again uses the netstrap and the terminator uses the mirror to remain in the middle of the probable angles of return. If balls are kept low, no angles are possible from the center of the court.

## Diagram 4
## Improper Positioning on a Center Ball Exposes the Middle

Neither the crosscourt player nor the terminator believes that they should position themselves so close together when the ball is so close to the center line. Balls will likely go through the middle for winners.

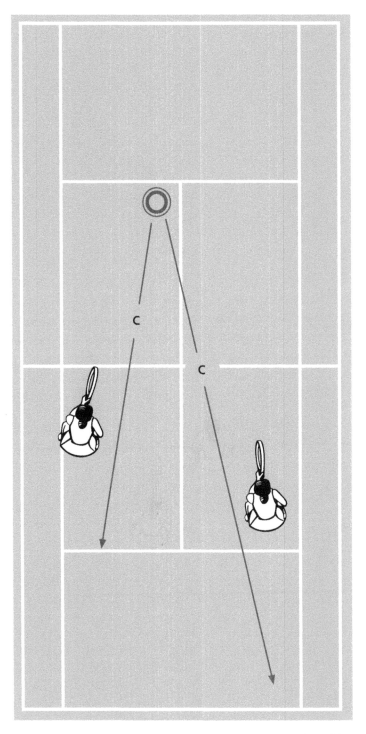

*The Art of Doubles*

one back" duo, then your team should know unequivocally that you are going to get lobbed. The crosscourt player should remain on the service line, and the terminator should assume a position several feet farther from the net in hopes of snagging a short lob. *You still control the net even though neither of you is "on" it.* The rule for the terminator is "two steps back and crunch." Beyond those two steps, the ball belongs to the crosscourt player. Remember that jobs do not overlap. One of the hardest things to explain to very talented athletes is that in this system, it is never whether you *can* ta ke a ball; the issue is whether you *should* take a ball. One player trying to do both jobs ruins the division of labor that makes this system unique.

If, however, your opponents are net rushers, then the crosscourt player should be positioned about three feet inside the service line and the terminator about three feet from the net because the chances of lobs off the racquets of serve and volley players are greatly reduced.

• **Know your job and stick to it.** If your crosscourt player lobs in a *straight line*, whether as an offensive weapon or the result of an emergency, a legitimate change of jobs has been created. He becomes the terminator, and the terminator shifts back to the crosscourt position. Your identity is determined by whether the ball is on your side of the court or crosscourt from you.

In truth, the terminator is the cornerstone of the formation. By the angle of his body and his movement, he controls whether the court stays tightly closed or becomes vulnerable to attack. As an example, note the two different paths to the net taken by the receiver's partner in diagram five. The receiver has hit an excellent low and wide service return. The dotted line represents an incorrect angle to the net taken by the terminator. It has opened the middle of the court for the server's volley, well out of reach of the crosscourt player, who has positioned himself with the netstrap. If this happens often, the receiver isn't going to adhere to the netstrap principle for fear of losing the point in the middle of the court.

## Diagram 5
### The Terminator's Angle to the Ball as He Moves Forward is Crucial

If the terminator cuts toward the alley with too severe an angle, he has opened the middle. If he stays in the middle of the probable angles of return, the court remains closed.

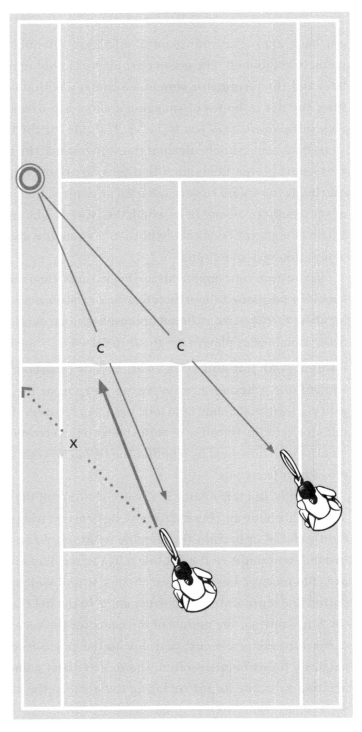

Yet, if he compromises that position, he is vulnerable on the angle. The solid line represents the proper angle to the net for the terminator, and the court remains impregnable.

The terminator may suddenly morph into an orange cone, never moving off the service line. In this case, it hardly matters what the poor crosscourt player does because his court has become a football field to cover. Perhaps the server's partner, who begins closer to the net than the receiver's partner, suddenly develops a serious case of baseline creep. Again, for every step backward this creeper takes, the crosscourt player's court widens further until it is an abyss. The most important job for the terminator is not putting the ball away or executing devastating poaches, but being a bookmark and keeping the crosscourt player's court to a manageable size.

• **Avoid the cardinal sin when you are the crosscourt player.** As a crosscourt player, you always have the right, or duty at times, to become the terminator *on the correct ball.* An inviolate rule for the crosscourt player is: *Never close the net and hit crosscourt.* If you are a crosscourt player and the lucky recipient of a short, juicy floater, you have the right and duty to close the net and put the ball away. But if you hit it crosscourt, you have created a situation where there are two terminators on your team, and your opponent's crosscourt lob will surely win the point. When you close, you must hit straight, making yourself the terminator and allowing your partner to back into crosscourt. If the ball comes back, your team is properly positioned. Sometimes those wily people across the net like to play "reel 'em in and lob 'em." You serve to Slippery Sly, and he dinks a ball to your side of the court. As you race to retrieve it, you must remember that he wants you to hit back crosscourt so he can lift the next ball right over your head in merciless glee. To foil him, you must play this ball in a *straight line,* either as a lob or a down-the-line shot, while your partner backs into crosscourt. Anytime you enter the terminator's purview on the court, *you must change the direction of the ball and hit in front of yourself.* It is not a perfect tennis world, but this offensive

DON'T TRY TO SNEAK BACK TO YOUR OFFENSIVE VOLLEY
POSITION ON A TEAM ALREADY ENTRENCHED AT THE NET. THEY WILL
VOLLEY BEHIND YOU. DIG IN AND PLAY DEFENSE.

court positioning covers your opponents' highest percentage shots and leaves them only with low percentage options. Your odds of prevailing in the match are very good.

## THE DEFENSIVE COURT POSITION

Sometimes your opponents' superior lobs are out of reach and force your team to retreat to the baseline. Occasionally, you may choose to play from the baseline. In either case, proper court position dictates that you *both* retreat. Never leave your partner at the net while you chase a lob or choose to stay back on the baseline. He is the prime target for the onrushing team's bone-crushing overhead. Be advised that this constitutes grounds for dumping you.

*The Art of Doubles*

The crosscourt player will run down the deep lob and call his partner back to the baseline with him. He should never try to drive the ball back across the net but rather execute as a high a lob as he can—a defensive lob—because his partner needs time to reach the baseline. Also, drives are the things your opponents angle off for winners when they have taken the net away from you. Once safely ensconced in your defensive position, lob every ball unless you see a gaping hole. The higher your lob, the more difficult it is for the interlopers across the net to angle anything in front of you. Be patient and try to have as much fun defending the court as you experience attacking it from the net. Both players have crosscourt and terminator duties from the baseline as well as the net. If you are crosscourt from a player hitting an overhead, retreat as far into the corner of the court on the diagonal as you can, and use the netstrap. If you are opposite a player hitting an overhead, mirror him precisely, and step to within a foot of the baseline. This way, your team has nearly all of the court covered. The crosscourt player takes the deep overhead on the angle, and the terminator takes the down-the-middle overhead (see diagram six).

Be sure to adjust jobs if your next lob drifts toward the other player. Remember that you can hit lobs a lot longer than they can hit overheads. The goal is to provoke them into overhitting or becoming irritated with the number of balls you can retrieve. If you persevere and remain committed to this strategy, it does work, and they will lose their tempers and hit the back fence.

You cannot reclaim the net just because you are bored with hitting lobs. Realize that one of you has to get to the crosscourt position, and one of you has to get to the terminator position before the ball is struck across the net, not to mention the perils of running into someone's overhead aimed at your face. The only way to regain the net is to lob behind your opponents and make them chase down the ball. This creates the time you need to get organized in your formation. Of course, if they hit you a very short ball, you must run in to retrieve

## Diagram 6
## Proper Defensive Court Position Against an Overhead Smash

By using the netstrap and stepping way beyond the baseline, the crosscourt player retrieves deep and angled overheads. The terminator remains opposite the player hitting the overhead and takes balls hit up the center of the court.

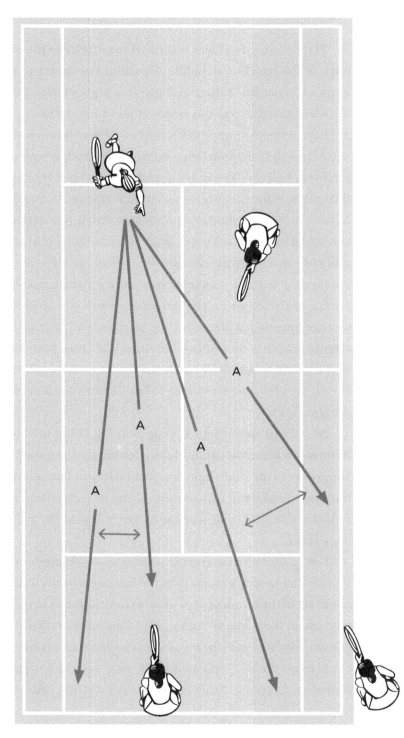

*The Art of Doubles*

it, but if you are both scrambling to reach a drop volley, it means you didn't lob high enough, and it is unlikely that you will gain control of the situation.

The real secret to executing a wonderful defensive lob is to think that you are going to hit it very high, but *let them hit it*. If you try to lob *over* them, it is almost always out. If you think that you are going to let them hit it, you will get your height, and if you are lucky, it *will* go over their heads and bounce. Then you have won back the net.

- **Know when to relinquish the net voluntarily.** There are times when purposely playing from the baseline is necessary. Suppose you are in a dogfight of a match, and the player whose serve you have not come close to breaking is about to step up to serve. If you both retreat to the baseline and lob all of your returns (and then follow the above rules), it upsets his rhythm. His targets are gone, his first volley is replaced by an overhead, and the pace of the match has slowed considerably. Very often it is just enough to encourage him to get anxious, angry, and overplay his shots. If it works, be sure to do it again next time he serves. Have you ever played a match in which it seemed as if all you did was blink and suddenly you're down 4-0? Retreating to the baseline will allow you both to slow down, take a few deep breaths, and recover your balance. After you have a foot in the door and have regained some confidence, you can return to attacking the net. There are also times when you may not be having difficulty with some brute's killer serve, but your partner is, and all of his returns are being poached off. It is a good idea to use the defensive formation when your partner receives, perhaps just on the first serve. It frees him to return from deeper in the court and lob the ball instead of feeling the pressure of having to squeeze a perfect return past the looming poacher.

The defensive formation should be as much a part of your repertoire as your offensive position. One of the most difficult things to teach my students is that you cannot be on offense in tennis all the time. Knowing when to retreat and how to retreat without hubris is smart tennis. Lobbing from the baseline shouldn't be your first choice in court position, but it should be one in which you are thoroughly proficient. It could salvage a victory for your team.

• **Nothing is more important than proper court position.** If position in life is everything, then court position in doubles is certainly everything. Do not cheat it by thinking that you can get away without it, for without it, you will seldom win. Do not neglect it by blaming a weak second serve for your wish not to take the net, because superior court position will often allow you to steal a match against technically superior opponents. Court position is the one thing that is entirely under your control. If you control your environment, you create options for your team, and intelligent shot selection is predicated on having numerous options.

Learning a new system of court positioning can be exasperating and arduous. Initially, it requires that you think much more about where you are on the court than you ever did before. While you are in the early stages of mastery, your game will suffer and you will be appalled that you cannot execute shots that were routine before you started this complicated process. This is normal and means you are really trying to change your old habits. It *will* go away. Enjoy the process without hurrying the finished product, and know that it is difficult to commit to strange geometrical thoughts about doubles. If it weren't so difficult, everybody would be good at it, and that would be no fun at all.

---

## Court Position Checklist

☐ The crosscourt player uses the netstrap and is the "worker bee." He sets things up for his terminator and is content to let the terminator bask in the glory of putting the ball away.

☐ The terminator employs the "mirror" concept and is responsible for ending the point.

☐ The offensive court position adjusts according to the opponents' formation.

☐ The defensive court position is necessary and requires patience.

☐ It takes time to master difficult concepts.

---

# 4

# Win With Intelligent Shot Selection

·····························

*It is circumstance and proper timing that give an action its character and make it either good or bad.*

·····························

***Agesilaus II***

Most ill-advised shot selection is due to a player's desire to end a point much too early. Every tennis point has a beginning, a middle, and an end. While your opponent may do you the favor of making an error early on, most points that you successfully complete must be won in stages. Inexperienced, aspiring teams, along with the "watchers" and "wonderers," fail to comprehend that the rules of tennis are written with the presumption that the ball will be returned and that there are people out there who can and will handle your best shot. Great doubles teams recognize this state of affairs as unavoidable and actually look forward to the challenge of a long rally, whereas "hoping no one will get to the ball" seems to be the prime motivation for unintelligent shot selection.

The beginning of a point includes only the serve and service return. The middle of the point extends from the first volley through all subsequent shots played, up to the one that will end the point. The end of the point is simply the one ball that does not come back into play. Players lacking in confidence or those who become overanxious tend to try to reverse this order and generally make a high number of unforced errors. Experienced doubles teams know they must be equally as intelligent in their choice of shots for the beginning of the point as they are for both the middle and the end of the point.

## PERCENTAGE TENNIS

High-percentage shot selection or "straight vanilla," as I say to my students, can be defined as using the best and most appropriate speed, spin, and direction on any ball given your distance from the net, the height of the ball you must play, and your opponents' court positions. It includes careful consideration of the score and where the momentum of the match lies. It is always the shot that, under the circumstances, has the highest probability of clearing the net and landing in the court. It is *never* the shot hit with the idea in mind that, "By God, this sucker's not coming back!"

## THE BEGINNING STAGE

In the beginning of the point (serve and service return), the server has an easier job than the receiver because he may choose to start the point any way he wishes, hopefully to his advantage. For example, serving with the score tight and the momentum in the balance is not the time to showcase a cannonball. Nor is it the time for a Wiffle ball accompanied by a prayer that the opponent will err. A high-percentage shot would be a three-quarter-speed serve placed deep and *down the middle* because a wide serve gives the receiver a better opportunity to hit a sharply angled return. If you are the receiver on a very important point, now is not the time to be a hero and unleash a down-the-line passing shot in hopes of grabbing the point quickly while no one is looking. Stick to your "bread and butter," which should be a short-angled cross-court. If, however, the speed, spin, or height of the serve is suddenly more than you bargained for, don't stubbornly stick to a plan that is no longer likely to succeed. Recognize the emergency, and use a defensive lob. If you play the deuce court and your right-handed partner is in the ad court, consider that an excellent high-percentage play is a deep lob into the alley behind the net player—the server's partner (see diagram seven). After the lob, move *all the way to the net*, to what my students call the "nose-on-net" position. Your partner should drift about three steps back from the service line and prepare to smash an overhead to your side of the court. About 90 percent of the defensive lobs returned to you from that corner come directly to your racquet or to the spot where your ad-court partner is waiting. If your partner is a leftie and plays the deuce court, you can create the same situation for him by using an offensive lob from the ad court.

Remember, the goal is to reach the middle of the point, but that is not possible if you don't get your service return in play.

## THE MIDDLE STAGE

Once you reach the middle of the point, both of you must realize that your distance from the net and your opponent's court positions dictate your targets and responsibilities. The middle of the point can become frantic, allowing little time for quick decisions, and not knowing the proper direction in which to hit the ball can cause unforced errors.

Determining where to play shots and in which direction can be condensed into the Deep to Deep, Short to Short Axiom (see diagram eight). Doubles teams lose more points because of their failure to understand or implement this formula than they do for all other reasons combined. The four rules of this axiom are:

1. Never play a ball "deep to short." (Usually applies to the crosscourt player.)
2. Always play balls "deep to deep." (Usually applies to the crosscourt player.)
3. Play balls "short to short" whenever you can hit down and punish the "short" opponent, overheads included. (Usually applies to the terminator.)
4. Play balls "short to deep" to keep your team out of trouble when hitting down is not an option. (Usually applies to the terminator.)

## Diagram 7
### The Deep Lob: A High-Percentage Play

The deuce court player should use the offensive lob as a service return. Be sure to follow it to the "nose on net" court position and allow your ad court partner to smash the overhead.

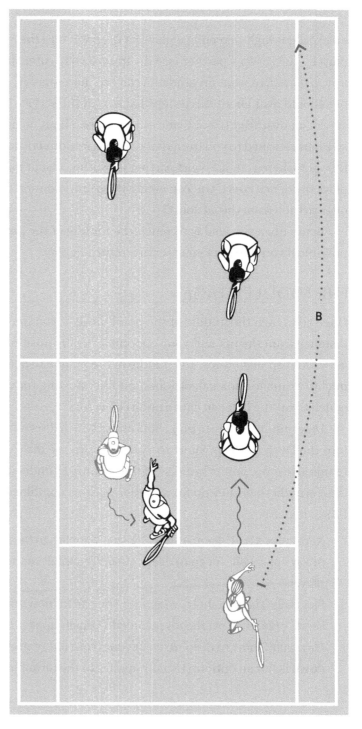

*The Art of Doubles*

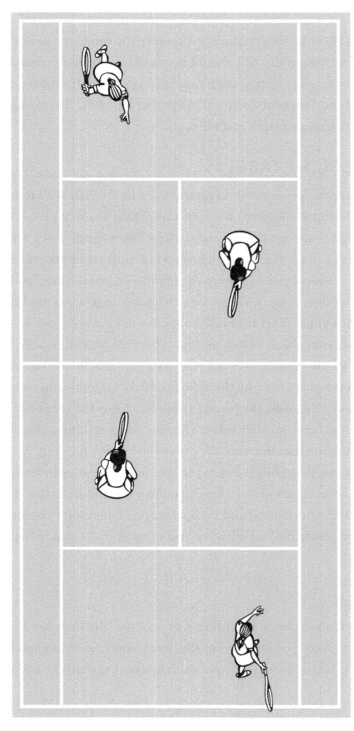

## Diagram 8
## The Deep to Deep, Short to Short Axiom

Looking at the diagram, imagine that you, the server, move toward the net and are about to strike your first volley. Your partner is in the terminator position. Across the net, the receiver's partner moves toward the terminator position, but the receiver remains near the base line. Both your partner and the receiver's partner are close enough to the net to hit down on any ball having sufficient net clearance to do so; thus their court positions may be defined as "short." You, the server, as well as the receiver, are both far enough away from the net that hitting down on any ball, regardless of its height, will send it into the net (overheads are the exception). If your distance from the net precludes your hitting down on a high volley or any ball that has bounced, your court position may be defined as "deep." It is a cardinal sin to play a ball "deep to short" since, in all probability, you will be hitting your shot with a trajectory rising up to an opponent's racquet poised to hit down at your vulnerable partner.

The Deep to Deep, Short to Short Axiom will remove the tendency to hesitate and think about where the ball should be played—a primary reason easy volleys are misplayed. "Deep to deep" will keep you out of trouble and "short to short" will end the point for you at the proper moment. This axiom is fully explained in diagrams eight and nine.

## AIM FOR THE RIGHT TARGETS

What if both opponents are camped on their service line? What if all four of you have gained proper offensive court position? Deep *people* and short *people* are not targets, nor are their racquets. The "deep-short" rules are only directional cues to indicate which targets on the court are appropriate in a given situation. "Short to short," "down the middle," "down the line," and "deep to deep" are all directions, within which there are targets. No matter how well you crunch your "short to short" volley, if you hit a good player's racquet, the ball will come back—often over your head for a clean winner.

Playing high-percentage tennis is not just having the ability to choose the proper direction, but also having the ability to strike targets accurately within that direction. First of all, the primary target is *always* the grass, clay, or asphalt—the *ground* on the other side of the net—not anything a player wears or carries. Bearing that in mind, the crosscourt player has only two possible targets for his first volley: either the ground in the alley in front of the other "deep," crosscourt player's shoes or down the middle to the "T" (the intersection of the horizontal and vertical service lines). Your choice of target should be predicated on whether you must play the inside ball or the outside ball.

### The Outside Ball

If you are a right-handed player executing a first volley (the first one for your team following return of serve) from the deuce court, your forehand volley is the outside ball and should be played crosscourt toward the deep

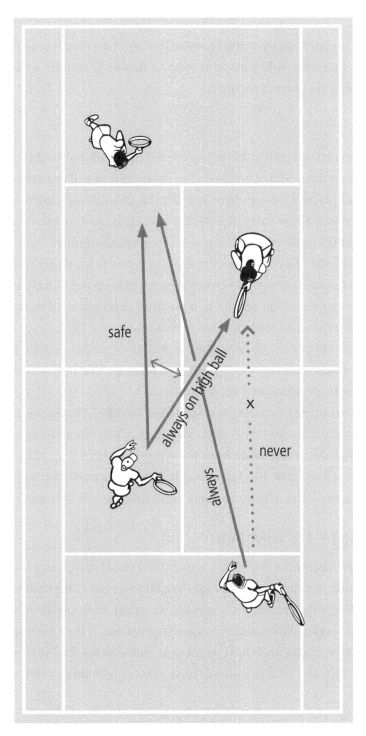

safe

always on high ball

always

x

never

### Diagram 9
## Court Scenario: Ball Direction and Placement

The ad court player in the foreground is in a short court position. He may safely play low balls back in the direction from which they have come ("short to deep") in order to keep his team out of trouble. He should punish high balls by playing them toward the opposing net player ("short to short") who will have very little time to react. He will be guilty of not ending a point in a timely fashion if he plays a high ball toward the opponent who is farther from the net (inappropriate time for the "short to deep" selection).

The deuce court player in the foreground is in a deep court position. His only option is to play all of his balls in the direction of the opponent who is farther from the net ("deep to deep"). If he has a mental lapse and hits toward the short opponent, his partner might be maimed for life and should divorce him. (Never play a ball "deep to short.")

opponent's shoes, and preferably angled toward his alley (see diagram ten). It is doubtful that this wide volley could be played down the middle without encountering the net player's racquet.

## The Inside Ball

If you must play a backhand volley, this is considered the inside ball and can be aimed safely down the middle because it has no angle and will not cross the plane of the net player's racquet before it hits the ground (see diagram ten). Never try to reverse these rules. The perils of doing so are illustrated in diagram eleven and fall under the heading of "no percentage tennis."

Remember that half volleys are perfectly legitimate shots for either ball and are always preferable to an out-of-balance lunge to keep the ball from bouncing. If for some reason you are not in a position to hit either of these shots well—if your sixth sense tells you that you are having an emergency—lob the net player. Never panic, abandon ship, and offer up a wounded duck to the opposition in hopes that they will blow an easy setup. That only works when your opponents are absolutely incompetent.

Lastly, adhere to the rule I impose on my students: "No CBS." That is, never get *cute, bored, or stupid.* The wee bit of court in the big guy's alley and the cute little piece of line on the extreme angle from you lying two inches beyond the net are the purview of rash fools. This is true on all shots, but is particularly applicable to first volleys (where a "deep-to-short" shot will lose you the point).

## OTHER TARGETS TO AIM FOR

Having successfully executed a first volley and gained your crosscourt player's offensive position, you have more targets available to you. Your choice of targets is totally dependent on your opponents' court position. If they are both back, then angles, dinks, and drops are appropriate. If they are one up and one back, then angles and short overheads aimed at the "up" player should be used. If they are "orange cones," those players who do not move

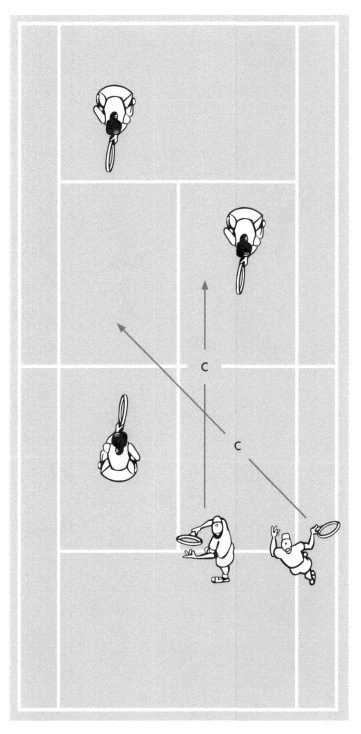

## Diagram 10
### Playing Inside and Outside Balls

The deuce court player should hit his forehand volley (the outside ball) crosscourt, and his backhand volley (the inside ball) through the middle of the court.

## Diagram 11
## The Dangers of Breaking the "Inside to Inside," "Outside to Outside" Rule

If the crosscourt player breaks the rules and plays his volley outside to middle, the opposing terminator will intercept it. If he attemps to play the volley middle to outside, there is not enough court and his ball will land wide.

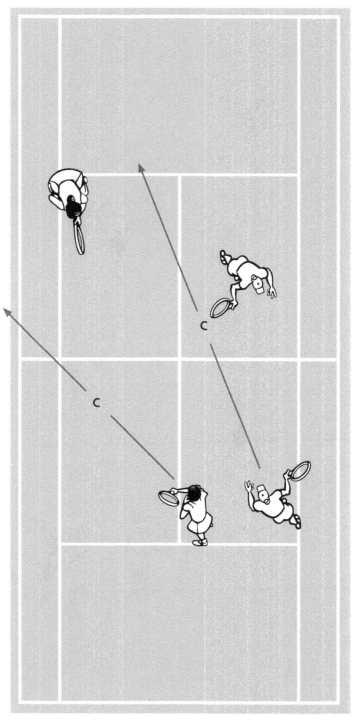

*The Art of Doubles*

but who possess great hands, use the middle. And if they are in just as good a net position as you are, you must adhere to the "inside-to-inside" and "outside-to-outside" rules (see diagrams forty-one to forty-four in chapter fourteen). Above all else, *do not hit back* to them, affording them an eternity to pick their shots.

## POACHING THE BALL

At any time in a point you are free to cross in front of your partner and intercept or "poach" a ball (be sure to move forward on the diagonal—not laterally). This refers to intercepting the ball in the middle of a point, perhaps after your crosscourt partner has executed several low volleys, forcing the other crosscourt player into a weak and floating volley. Poaching off your partner's serve is discussed at length in chapter five. When you make this poaching move, never choose the target lying in the alley on the side of the court you have just vacated. This error is called "hitting behind yourself"— moving in one direction and playing the ball back in the direction from which you came (see diagram twelve). An alert opponent will swiftly pick the ball up and send it down the line into the alley you have abandoned— an alley your partner has had no time to cross behind you and cover. If you meet up with the ball in the center of the court, choose the target at the "T." If you have passed the center of the court by the time you intercept the ball, choose the target in the alley toward which you are moving.

## CLOSING THE NET

"Closing the net" allows the terminator to use sharply angled volleys and play his shots into parts of the court unavailable to him from his normal position about four feet from the net. Closing the net increases the chance that the volley will be a putaway and not just a pathetic little wounded volley. The trick is to recognize when that option is present and to take advantage of it immediately.

## Diagram 12
### Avoid Hitting Behind Yourself

Never move to the right and play your volley to the left, or vice versa. If you hit "behind yourself," an alert opponent will take the ball down your line for a winner.

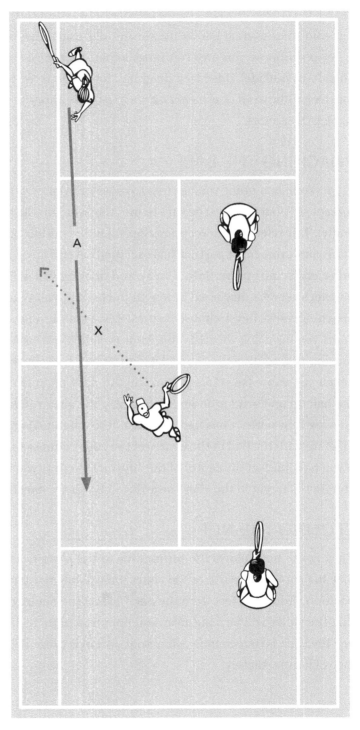

*The Art of Doubles*

Not long ago I was teaching a lesson in which the students in the terminator position were asked to recognize the soft, floating ball and instantly smother it by closing the net. The lesson was not going well. Exasperated, I finally asked, "For heaven's sake, what *is* a 'floater,' anyway?" One of the women timidly replied, "Well, I think it's a ball that used to be something else."

Although she was not completely accurate, this woman did have the right idea. Most balls that are mis-hit (struck off the frame or "dug out"), and therefore carry unintentional spin, end up "floating" across the net. Also, balls hit when a player is forced into a very awkward posture will often float.

You must learn to recognize floaters not only by watching your opponent's racquet, but also by listening for that off-center sound of the mis-hit ball. Once you identify that juicy opportunity, close on the ball quickly and take advantage of your job as terminator by rifling your volleys at extremely sharp angles. This move will not only allow you to play balls toward your alley targets, but also your proximity to the net will give you the opportunity to hit a piece of ground well in front of the opposing terminator (see diagram thirteen).

## MAKING LOW-PERCENTAGE TENNIS PAY OFF

"Low-percentage tennis" can be defined as hitting shots that disregard the most appropriate speed, spin, or direction for a given situation. Instead, a player selects a target or a racquet speed that allows far less margin for error but carries the element of surprise. In certain situations, the psychological edge gained by successfully executing these low-percentage shots is worth the risk.

If yours is the receiving team and the server is down 0-40, it is an excellent time to unveil the most powerful service return in your arsenal. You may not have the confidence to unleash it at any other time in the match, but your opponents won't know that and will begin to wonder what you might hurl at them next.

**Diagram 13**
## To Hit a Sharper Angle, the Terminator Must "Close" the Net

When the poaching terminator moves on a sharp diagonal, he can execute a very short-angled volley out of the reach of the opposing terminator.

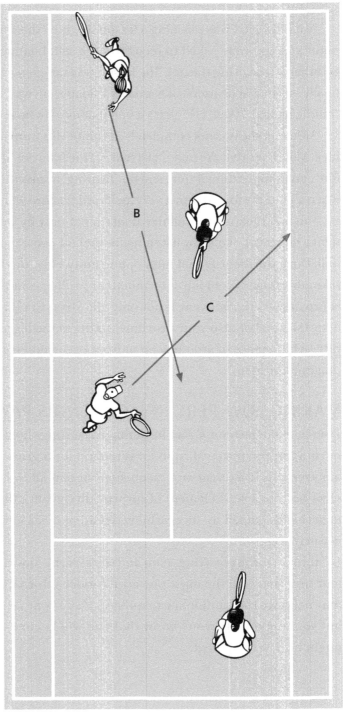

*The Art of Doubles*

Using low-percentage shot selection doesn't win matches, but it does make statements. When you are receiving serve at ad-out, the server is facing break point. He may double fault and lose his serve, for which he has only himself to blame, but if he *does* give his service game away, he also knows that winning it the next time is within his power. If, on the other hand, you, as the receiver, cause him to lose his serve by surprising him with a superb low-percentage lob volley for a winner, or a softly angled volley that wrong-foots him, he may well feel incapable of ever controlling his service game again.

Executing a high-risk shot successfully is not only a wonderful confidence builder for your team, but also a morale destroyer for your opponents. Great doubles players know when the time is right and will not hesitate to try a very difficult shot, even in a tiebreak. Bear in mind that a tiebreak is designed to be close, and you should not panic if you fail to leap to a 6-0 lead. If you find yourself receiving serve at 5 points all in a tiebreak, you should consider this a good time to surprise your opponents with your guts and courage by trying to make a clean winner. If you make it, your team serves for the set on the very next point. If you miss it, you are still "on serve" and should work hard to hold both your service points. Meanwhile, you have probably scared your opponents to death with your ability to be courageous under pressure.

## KNOW WHEN TO BAIL OUT OF A SHOT

Experienced doubles teams know when to pressure their opponents with low-percentage shot selection, when to play high-percentage tennis, and just as important, when to bail out. What may seem like an intelligent choice of shots when you are balanced and poised to strike is always a bad idea if you suddenly find that your body is not centered over your feet. Differentiate between risk taking, which has a reasonable probability of success, and failing to bail out, which has virtually no probability of success. If you plan to hit your service return down your opponent's line in a most convincing manner, but suddenly find the serve unexpectedly forcing, your original idea is no longer plausible. Rather than stubbornly sticking to it, you should immediately bail out, choosing instead to play a defensive lob. Failure to do so is not high-risk tennis; it is mindless disregard for an emergency.

Using high-risk shots when you are not playing well is a formula for disaster. If you can't make the routine "vanilla" shots on a given day, you most certainly won't make the high-risk shots. It might take longer, but stick patiently to your high-percentage arsenal.

Resist the temptation to be a hero. If the situation calls for a high-percentage safe volley, make it. Don't let the dreams of cheers and applause for the unbelievably impossible winner cloud your vision. Above all, learn to be comfortable with the knowledge that the end of the point is simply the one ball that you expected to come back, but didn't. Your team will have truly arrived when you begin to view the last ball as a disappointment rather than a relief.

Finally, don't get cute, bored, stupid, stubborn, fancy, or greedy. Webster defines *intelligent* as "having knowledge, understanding and awareness." A truly intelligent doubles team must have all of that, tinged with generous doses of discretion, patience, and superior racquet work.

## THE SHOTS YOU NEED

To play great doubles, it is essential that you master the ability to hit certain shots. And it is a waste of your time and money to learn others. The shots you must include in your repertoire include:

### The Half Volley

Players spend too much time turning up their noses at the half volley and lose too many points trying to avoid it. This is largely because its execution

*The Art of Doubles*

is confusing. The half volley is played off a ball that has struck the court but *must be volleyed anyway.* Players try to use a groundstroke to execute the shot when, in fact, the stroke production should precisely replicate that of a volley. The fact of the matter is that the half volley is the most important shot in doubles, so you must give up your reluctance and embrace it. Whether or not you need to play a half volley, rather than a low volley, is entirely a function of the expertise of the service returner. You can neither run skidding on your nose to keep it from bouncing nor back up and let the ball bounce so that you can use a full ground stroke. The good news is that if you can hit a low volley, you can hit a half volley because they are played in exactly the same way. The bad news is that you must learn to keep it low enough that it bounces in front of the other crosscourt player. If it bounces for you and doesn't bounce for him, he is going to hit down at your defenseless terminator.

## A Spin Serve

You need to serve up the middle so that your partner has an opportunity to poach on the return. But if all you have is a flat serve, you are in serious trouble. All the best service returners love to get their hands extended without moving their feet. If all you have is a flat serve up the middle, then this serve may well be the ball that lands in a good returner's "roundhouse," the area of the court where he can plant his feet and tee off on the ball, perhaps knocking you onto your rear. The slice serve (assuming you are a right-handed player) will jump to an opponent's right. Toss the ball to your right and hit the *right side* of the ball only. For topspin, the toss goes back over your head and to the left. Hit the *left side* of the ball only. This will make the ball kick up and jump to your opponent's left. Either topspin or slice will make the returner unable to set his feet. And he will have to play the ball at a less comfortable height. Spinning your serve allows you to remain in control of your first volley.

## An Excellent Array of Volleys

You can't just own *a* volley because your opponent doesn't just hit you *a* ball. So many times a player thinks of the volley as just one generic stroke when in fact each player must own a wide array of volleys. No other stroke demands such diversity.

You must be able to respond to the variety of strokes aimed at you from various places on the court with different volleys. You need deep, ugly volleys as part of your defense against the lob queens (see chapter six). You need angle volleys against both the lob queens and the net-rushing teams. You need drop volleys (deft touch volleys that just barely clear the net) when you are the terminator and the player trying to drive the ball through you has stayed back. You need swinging volleys for a variety of circumstances, but most importantly, to handle the lob you have taken out of the air rather than allowing it to bounce (see chapter six). And finally, you need a lob volley (open the face of the racquet slightly to loft the ball over his head) to make those over eager crosscourt players pay when they have over-closed the net (remember that the *crosscourt* lob is the most devastating weapon you have). Be aware that a *two-handed* backhand volley is a huge liability. You cannot stretch well for wide shots, and you most definitely cannot handle balls hit directly at you without going through amazing contortions.

## A Creative Overhead

Many players think an overhead smash is just that—a ball crunched as hard as the player can swing. But those are the balls that the lob queens *re-lob* better than the last lob they hit. It is very important to own an angled overhead that you can aim inside the service line into either alley. These shots are totally out of the reach of the lob queens entrenched on the base-line, and they definitely shorten what would otherwise be a long day at the office. If you are a right-handed player, slice the overhead from the deuce court and use the idea of the topspin serve from the ad court. Execute these shots from as deep in the court as your expertise allows.

## A Slice Backhand

When you hit a backhand drive, you have to stop and plant your feet because you are swinging away from your body. All service returns are approach shots to the net, and all approach shots to the net are hit while the player is moving forward into position. You can move through a backhand slice because there is almost no body rotation associated with its execution. The preparation is exactly that of a volley, and knifing from high to low through the ball creates the underspin. If you can't slice your backhand, then you can't move through your return, and you will arrive in your crosscourt player's net position late—perhaps well behind the server's arrival. The most common result is that you will find yourself having to volley up to a server waiting to hit down. You can, of course, always move toward the net on your forehand *drive* because you are hitting toward your body. When you hit toward your body, you are hitting in the direction you are moving.

## A Dropshot

The most devastating weapon you have against incessant lobbers is a good dropshot. Their favorite event is to serve to you and wait for your low, hard, and deep drive to land in their timing space near the baseline (see chapter six). It is worth every hour you spend on the practice court to develop a reliable and delicate dropshot. Nothing you could do against them discomfits them more than this touch shot. They simply have no answer for it. The key to hitting a perfect dropshot is to recognize that you should use the stroke production of your volley to create underspin and make sure it has a great deal of height. Make sure that you keep the apex on *your side* because the higher it is on your side, the shorter it drops on their side.

## An Underspin Lob

If all you own is a "flat" lob, an abbreviated version of your drive, your options are limited. It is nearly impossible to hit a flat lob off a big serve because you can't control the ball on your strings well enough against that pace. You have to wait for a softer, second serve before you can hit a good offensive lob, and that might be a while. An underspin lob can be executed off *any* serve, will bounce and stop dead because of the spin, and will stay in the court in the wind. It is also an excellently disguised shot because it looks just like your dropshot and offensive crosscourt slice or chip return. Again, the stroke production mimics that of the volley.

## THE SHOTS YOU DON'T NEED

Before you spend thousands of dollars on lessons, ask yourself if you intend to be both a singles and a doubles player or if you intend to stick to doubles only. If you intend to become a doubles specialist, you shouldn't spend your money on shots more appropriate for the singles court, which include.

## Topspin Groundstrokes

These days you simply cannot compete on the singles court without owning topspin groundstrokes. If your opponent has them and you don't, you will spend the match clinging to the uppermost rungs of the back fence. But unless your mastery of topspin includes the ability to hit severely dipping angled service returns, your ball is going to be rising and gaining net clearance just as the server arrives in position to hit down on your ball on the doubles court. If topspin and extreme western grips are all you have, at least learn to flatten them out when returning serve. There is also the problem of having to make a radical grip change when you arrive at the net to volley. With rare exceptions, players will not be successful at the net without a continental grip.

## A Big, Flat Serve

If a spin serve is a necessity for your doubles game, then a big, flat serve is definitely not a good option. Not only does it allow good receivers to tee off, but it also significantly shortens the time you have to get set before the ball comes back. The idea of serving aces in doubles is folly. For every ace you hit, ten returns will come whizzing by your outstretched racquet faster than you can prepare to volley them.

## A Topspin Lob

If you already own a topspin lob, you are fortunate. But it is not worth the time and money for a doubles player to acquire one because its uses are so few. Hitting a topspin lob takes time, and you have to set your feet. Therefore you can't use it as a service return, because you need to be moving forward, and you can't use it as a server in place of your first volley—hopefully, that wouldn't occur to you. The only circumstance in which you could use it is when your team is in the defensive court position and you have the time to step into the shot and lift it over the net team's heads. Its use in doubles is too specialized to be of significant value.

## A Two-Handed Backhand

Two-handed backhands are superfluous in doubles. If you have one, then you can hit a very effective service return with it, but if you don't have one, don't bother to learn one unless you are suffering from extreme tennis elbow. All you really need is the one-handed slice. Also, players who hit their returns with two hands often struggle to take the non-dominant hand off the racquet and switch quickly to the one-handed backhand volley. Many players find it difficult to handle a high-bouncing kick serve to the backhand when they use two hands on the racquet.

Just as you carefully select the proper tennis clothes and the perfect racquet with that great feel, so should you make sure that you own all the stroke equipment that produces intelligent shot selection.

## Shot Selection Checklist

☐ Play the beginning, the middle, and the end of each point in order.

☐ Remember that mistakes you make in the beginning of a point are generally due to an unwillingness to play a long point.

☐ Mistakes you make in the middle of the point are often caused by not understanding the Deep to Deep, Short to Short Axiom (see page 48).

☐ Mistakes you make while trying to end the point result from not knowing where the targets on the court lie (see diagram thirteen).

☐ Use low-percentage, high-risk shots intelligently and only when the tenor of the match allows it.

☐ Make high-percentage tennis the rule, not the exception.

☐ Don't ever get CBS: *cute, bored or stupid.*

☐ Master the shots you need to play intelligent doubles.

☐ Forgo learning shots better suited to the singles court.

*The Art of Doubles*

# 5

# Develop Superior Poaching Skills

...................................

*It is only by risking our persons from one hour to another that we live at all. And often enough our faith beforehand in an un-certified result is the only thing that makes the result come true.*

...................................

**William James**

Sometimes the word "poaching" itself is enough to make my students break into cold sweats. When I give a lesson on this technique, the idea is usually met with sheepish grins, but in the students' eyes I read, "Oh my God, you're going to make me risk looking like a fool, and maybe I'll do it in this lesson to humor you, but you'll never catch me running across the net and putting my partner's ball in the bottom of the net in a match." Sometimes in their determination to conquer their fear of poaching, or "taking a partner's ball," they career across the net so fast they end up interrupting a point on the next court over, unable to put on the brakes in time. Sometimes they have to listen to their own recalcitrant servers admonish from behind them, "You know, if you ever took my ball in a match, I'd kill you." Sometimes they start to move across the net, swing wildly at the ball, change their minds, and retreat, after which they make a circle, turn around to see if their partners are there to play the ball, and ultimately throw up their hands and appeal to me in utter confusion.

A GREAT POACHER IS THE MOST INTIMIDATING FORCE A RECEIVER CAN FACE, BUT MAKING THE MOVE TAKES COURAGE, AND KNOWING WHEN AND HOW TO MOVE AND WHERE TO HIT THE BALL ARE SKILLS OF SOME INTRICACY.

If you and your partner choose *not* to be a signaling team (the advantages and disadvantages of signaling your poaches are discussed later in this chapter), then you, when playing the net, can become a menacing freelancer whose movement can destroy your opponents' ability to return serve.

## PLAN TO POACH

One of the secrets to becoming an accomplished poacher is to believe that you will have a chance to poach on every serve your partner hits and that you

*The Art of Doubles*

relish the opportunity. It doesn't always work out that way, but you should start with that assumption. You cannot defer to your server on every ball that crosses the net because there are three excellent reasons to poach:

1. Every time you poach a ball, you create a new and different angle. This causes the opposition to have to make rapid adjustments to a ball hit very sharply.
2. Poaching allows you to play a ball "short to short"—the most desirable target on the court (see chapter four).
3. You are an invaluable asset to your server. He will hit many fewer balls and be a lot less tired.

Just as your partner prepares to serve, assume your fierce posture in the middle of your service box. As you hear him hit the serve, move straight toward the net, all the while watching whether the receiver is preparing his racquet to hit an inside ball or an outside ball. You cannot poach on the outside ball (a right-hander's forehand in the deuce court, for example) because the angle of the crosscourt is running away from you. If the serve goes to the outside, honor your mirroring responsibilities and forget all thoughts of poaching. If, however, the serve is to the inside, you must move to the center line and cover the middle *at a minimum* (see diagram fourteen). This movement is *not* optional. It is like reading the instructions on the box. If you want to make a cake, you follow the directions on the box. At the center line, decide if you wish to encroach upon your partner's court and execute your poach. You are never obligated to cross the center line, particularly if you feel that the return is too fast, too low, or too wide. And yet you must believe that you will have a chance to intercept on each inside serve. The key to brilliant poaching is to realize that, as long as the move is not a signaled poach, you are under absolutely no obligation to go flying across the court into your partner's alley just because you have begun the move. It is not a mistake to change your mind at the netstrap. In fact, it is often prudent. The real mistake is to go lurching wildly into

## Diagram 14
### Be a Patient Poacher

Wide serves are not good to poach on because the angle of the crosscourt return is running away from you. Wait for or encourage your partner to serve up the middle so you can more easily intercept the angle and not have to guard your alley.

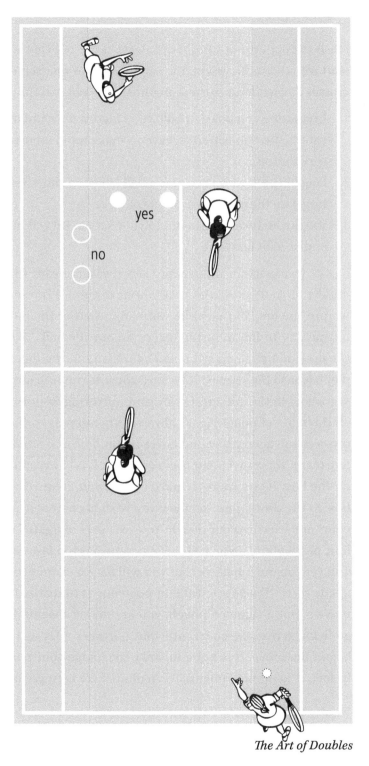

*The Art of Doubles*

your partner's court or to stop dead square in your partner's line of sight and turn around to look at him instead of getting out of the way.

## REASONS TO ABORT A POACH

Here are several legitimate reasons to stop your move in midflight and quickly sidestep back into your original position:

- If, having begun your poach, you see that the ball is hit hard and is headed for your partner's alley, you probably would never catch up with it. You should retreat.

- If you have crossed into your partner's court and find that, when the ball reaches you it is approximately level with the net or below it, step away and let the ball go through to your partner, who should have an easier play by virtue of his distance from the net.

- If your opponents play your partner's serve very early and from very close to the service line, it may also be taken on the rise. In this case, too, you should retreat because you have no time to react to the ball.

- In general, withdraw from balls angling sharply away from you, balls hit so hard that you can't react in time, and balls crossing the net too low to punish.

If you follow these guidelines, you will be highly successful in putting away those balls you do choose to intercept. Once you understand which balls you should take and which balls you should let go through to your partner, your movement will become confident and fluid, and you can begin to improvise.

## STRATEGIES FOR POACHING

- Imagine that your partner serves wide to the player in the ad court. Having first discharged your mirroring responsibility by covering your alley, you realize that while the service return is angling away from you, it is a slow-moving, high "sitter." Go get it! The speed and height of the ball present no problems for you, so the floater can belong to you if you want it. A great poacher will always want it.

- Suppose the player in the deuce court returns serve so well that you have yet to get your racquet on one of his returns. Ask your partner to hit a wide serve. Then, try feigning a rather disinterested posture to make the receiver believe you have lost concentration. Just *before* the player prepares to strike his return, make a fake move to poach and immediately move to cover your alley. Many times this ploy will draw an attempt to pass you in your alley, for which you are absolutely prepared. Although technically this is *not* a poach, it *is* one more ball that you, not your server, plays, and every time you help him out, he will be grateful. Don't forget to smile as you volley a winner between your two stunned opponents.

- Another successful tactic employed by excellent poachers is to vary the starting court position. The first thing a receiver does when he prepares to return serve is note the server's partner's court position. Eliminate two of the receiver's serve-return options by positioning yourself close enough to the serve lines to discourage the lob and near enough to your alley to prevent a down-the-line shot. Your stance will often generate the crosscourt return you are looking to poach. If you do assume this position, adjust forward and to the center of your court as soon as you hear your partner serve. Otherwise, you will have too much court to cover for a successful poach. Remember that this position is a fake, assumed only to encourage the receiver to hit the shot you want him to hit.

- Similarly, if you begin the point with your nose hanging over the net, you are encouraging the lob—an excellent kind of fake for those who love to hit overheads. Again, remember to adjust out of your fake as you hear the serve being struck.

Constant variety in starting court positions is an advantage because the tactic tends to drive receivers crazy. Invent your own ways of distracting and otherwise harassing the receiving team. It is one of the most satisfying aspects of good doubles.

## WHERE TO HIT A POACH

Knowing *where* to hit your poaches is just as important as knowing *if* you should take the ball (remember—don't go on the outside serve). All the great movement in the world is of no value if you do not execute your volley to a proper target, and playing the ball in the wrong direction on a poach is definitely grounds for your partner to divorce you.

Always play the ball in the direction you are moving *and make sure to follow it*. You should end up directly in front of the ball you hit. This will allow your partner ample time to cross behind you. Of course, all poaches are not putaways, even though we would like them to be, and failure to follow your poach is the biggest cause of lost points on poaches that come back. If you, as the terminator, and your partner, as the crosscourt player, do not switch courts, the entire center of your court is open for the opposing terminator's return volley (see diagram fifteen).

If you meet up with the ball in the center of the court, play the volley down the middle to the "T" so that the ball hits the ground, and remain in front of it. Your partner will not cross behind you in this situation. If you have crossed the center service line, choose the target in the alley toward which you are moving. Keep in mind that the closer you are to the net when you hit the ball, the more likely you will be successful. If you have begun your move on a serve to the deuce court opponent, your target is your ad court opponent's alley; if you began moving on the ad court opponent, your target is your deuce court opponent's alley (see diagram sixteen). Remember that the targets are in the respective opponent's alleys on the ground—*not* the sweet spots of their racquets. While it is true that occasionally you can hit hard enough at a player to intimidate him, good doubles players will not flinch and will often try to volley off your poach for a winner. But if you and your partner have successfully switched sides, your court should be fairly impregnable (see

## Diagram 15
### Not Following Your Poach Opens the Middle of the Court

If the poaching terminator does not follow his poach and enable his partner to cross behind him, he has left the entire middle of the court open for the opposing terminator's volley.

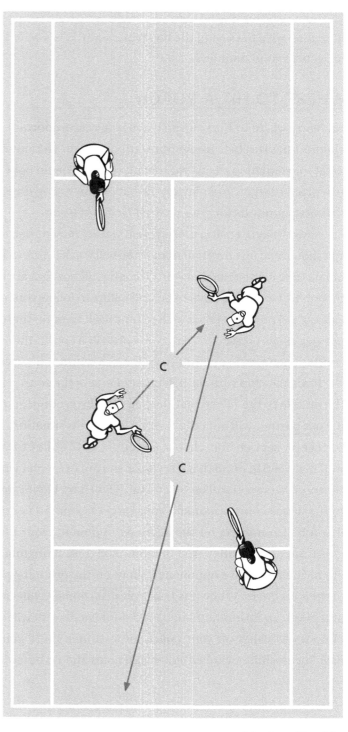

*The Art of Doubles*

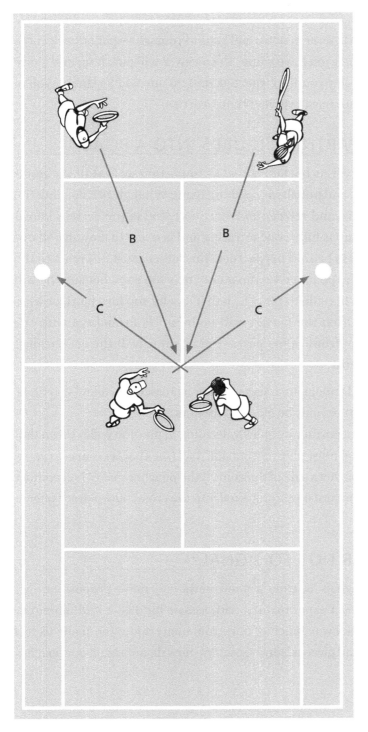

## Diagram 16
### Targets for Poaching

If you poach from the deuce court, your target lies in the deuce court opponent's alley. If you poach from the ad cout, your target lies in your ad court opponent's alley.

diagram seventeen). *Never* poach a ball behind yourself—that is, back in the direction from which you have come. The receiver will pick it up and shove it right down the alley you have vacated, and no one will be there—you've left and your partner hasn't yet had time to arrive.

## HOW YOUR PARTNER FIGURES INTO A POACH

The role of the server as backup is just as important as that of the terminator on a smooth and polished poaching team. What gives a poacher the confidence to move and retreat and start and stop is the certain knowledge that his backup is fully concentrating and is ready to play all balls, or, if necessary, to cross behind his partner. The server must not react to the first few steps of the poacher. He must not cross too soon because he will have to remain on his side to play the ball if it is hit too low, hard, or wide for the poacher. Often the players will be in an "I" formation, with the poacher literally in front of his partner momentarily. If the server must play the ball, he must:

1. Be quick-witted enough to assess whether a crosscourt volley is possible because his partner may be blocking the shot.
2. Avoid hitting his partner by quickly deciding to play the volley down the center, even if he must play the "outside" ball (see chapter four).
3. Cross to the poacher's side of the court if the poacher makes ball contact. Always move forward on the diagonal into the crosscourt player's offensive position.

## TO SIGNAL OR NOT TO SIGNAL?

Using poaching signals is truly a good news/bad news proposition. My doubles partner and I experimented with signals for a year and ultimately decided that it took away much of our spontaneity and often made us feel "rooted" when we had given a "stay" signal. We now do not signal our poaches

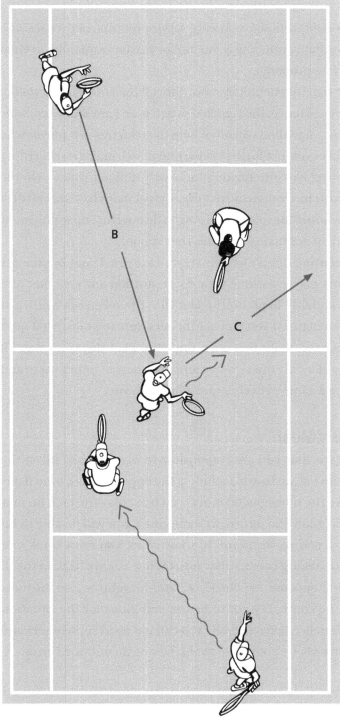

**Diagram 17**

## The Server's Job When a Partner Poaches

If a poacher plays the ball, he must follow it, crossing in front of his partner. The server must fill in on the side vacated by the poacher and remain in his crosscourt position. The terminator has changed the direction of the ball, but he remains in front of it. The jobs of each player remain unchanged.

B

C

against tough opponents who have forcing service returns, but we *will* use them against teams that continuously lob us (for reasons explained in chapter six on covering lobs properly).

Using poaching signals is definitely more difficult than freelancing volleys. Unlike the spontaneous move, the signaled poach is an irrevocable commitment to cross the net. Signaling will often help the reluctant net player who would otherwise never venture forth to experiment with uncharted territory, but it also forces the player into making some very difficult volleys. On the other side of the question, freelancing requires a great many last-second decisions, and players who are inexperienced or who do not trust their judgment will sometimes end up not taking the balls they should.

The mere fact of using signals usually serves to distract your opponents. When you, as the net player, assume your court position and give that first hand signal, you can fairly bank on the fact that the receiver's heart just skipped a beat. Even better if you can get the receivers to guess what your signals mean—"Let's see, that's two 'goes,' one 'stay.' I bet this is a 'go' so I'll try a return into the alley." By then they've forgotten how to return serve and are now just playing a game of twenty questions with you.

## What the Signals Mean

A signaled "go" means that you are responsible to play all balls hit in the direction you are moving, up to and including the opposite alley, even if it is a wide serve. Unlike the nonsignaled move, you *must* play the ball, no matter how hard, wide, or low the return. In some cases, you will be able to hit down to your target, ending the point. In some cases, you must think of it as starting the point, taking care to play difficult low volleys back in the direction from which they came, or "blocking" hard-hit returns into the most accessible part of the court. Try not to be too ambitious for the situation, recognizing the difference between balls you can put away for winners and balls that must be handled carefully to avoid making an unforced error.

It is not necessary to serve down the middle on a signaled poach. You and your partner should decide whether a receiver's forehand or backhand return would give the poacher the maximum opportunity to intercept. Perhaps an ad court player wails his forehand but slices his backhand. In this case, the poacher has a better chance of catching up to the backhand than the forehand. However, there is a caveat for the server: If you said you were going to serve wide to that ad court player's backhand, then the serve *must go where you said it would* or you need to make sure it is a fault. This is your protection for the poacher. You cannot say, "Oops, it went to the forehand by mistake." You might get your terminator terminated.

When signaling a "stay," be careful not to abdicate all responsibility for a ball whizzing by your ear. You still have your mirroring responsibilities, and you should still be looking to poach a wounded-duck return. You are still the terminator on your team, and you must still look to intercept very weak returns. "Staying" does not mean total stagnation. It means being aware and alert.

Although it is always the terminator giving the signal, as server, you always have the right to contradict the signal and ask for a different one. Because your responsibility is to be deadly accurate and put the serve where you said you would, you should negate the "go" signal if you are not particularly confident in your accuracy on a given day. If you are tired or out of breath and want help, refuse the "stay" by simply saying "no," and your partner should respond by flashing you the "go" (poach) signal that you are looking for.

When using signals, as the terminator, you may begin your move a second earlier than if it were a nonsignaled poach because your partner is automatically crossing behind you and the entire court should be covered. The server should take care to move forward on the diagonal, his goal being to assume the crosscourt position on the side you have vacated. This is a difficult move for the server because he has a great deal of court to cover to position himself for the potential "down-the-line" return. For this reason, he should bear in mind that, if he does serve wide, he will have very little time to gain his offensive volley position and nab the "down-the-line" return, which will reach his side of the court very quickly and without an angle.

Another problem for the signaling team is the "down-the-middle" service return. Once the server has put the ball in play, there can be no change of plan when using signals. If you are a right-handed player moving across the net in a point served to the deuce court, you cannot halt your progress across the net, stop, and reach back to a backhand volley since this freezes your team in an "I" formation and is tantamount to changing the plan. Your server, who expects you to be well across the center service line at this point, is poised to play the ball. If you change directions to stab at a volley, neither side of the court is covered, and neither of you knows where to go next. As terminator, you must have the discipline to let all balls that are hit behind you go through to the server and stick to the plan, which is that your movement across the net is continuous and should not be interrupted (see diagram eighteen).

## How to Signal

Many players use a clenched fist behind the back for a "stay" signal and an open palm for a "go" signal, re-signaling between first and second serves when the first serve is a fault. As a server, I find this distracting and prefer my partner to use one signal per point—one finger pointed down if he is only going on the first serve, two fingers pointed down if he intends to go on both serves, or the clenched fist if he is "staying." In all cases, the server must verbally acknowledge the signal before serving, or the net player cannot be sure the server knows which play has been called.

When accepting your partner's signal, always use the same words and tone of voice no matter which signal has been given. Two of my students came to me not long ago and complained that their poaches never really worked because it seemed that somehow the opponents *always* knew whether they were "going" or "staying." After much investigation, we discovered that when one of the team members was the server, she would acknowledge her

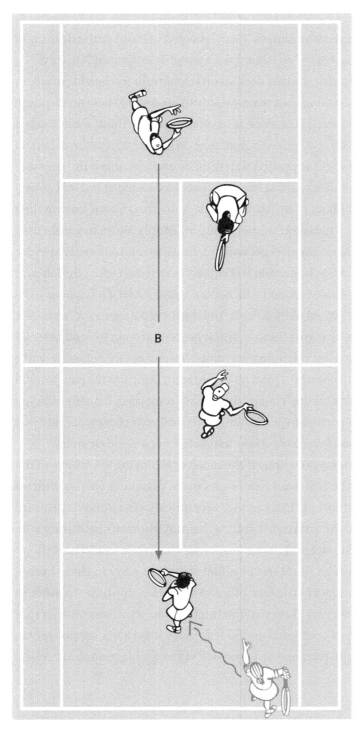

**Diagram 18**

## A Signaled Poach Requires Discipline

When poaching, remember that a signaled "go" cannot be aborted when the ball is in flight. Have the discipline to continue across the net and let the server pick up all balls hit behind you.

B

partner's "stay" signal with a simple "Yeah," uttered without enthusiasm, and she answered her partner's "go" signal with a highly animated "Oh-kay!"

Whether your team eventually decides on signaling or freelancing or a combination of both, it is vital to your team's ability to hold serve that you *do* poach because the intimidation factor alone is beyond measure. Think about the last time you played a team that moved a great deal on your service returns. Do you actually remember how many poaches they made and how many they missed? Or do you just remember wishing like hell that they would stand still so you could return serve? Many of my students are so worried about leaving their alleys uncovered for a potential winner that they simply refuse to vacate their position—ever. Somehow they feel personally humiliated and defeated if they are passed in the alley. I wish they would feel equally as defeated when the lob sails over their heads. Anybody can, and will, make a winner. And if it happens to be one struck into your vacant alley, so be it. You don't even have to say "nice shot," or even notice the smirk across the net. Simply get on with your job and never let a passing shot or two deter you from poaching. The rewards are definitely worth the work it requires to become a good poaching team. And if, in the end, you still do not feel comfortable taking "your partner's ball," remember that any time you cross in front of your partner to play a shot, you cut off your opponents' recovery time substantially, and you create a new and better angle for your volley.

Some final words on poaching: If the receiver is playing his return on the rise, that is before the ball even reaches its peak, poaching will be difficult because the ball will come off his racquet very quickly. If he is moving toward the net diligently as he strikes his return, he may shorten the distance between his point of impact and his target across the net. It would be difficult to move quickly enough to intercept a ball struck so early in time. Even if you become discouraged in the face of these obstacles, continue to move to the center line on every inside serve. You might get lucky. Also, consider that the higher the level of competition, the less likely it is that a service return will come floating the terminator's way looking like a big grapefruit. And it is often the case in women's tennis that players return serve better than they can serve. Therefore, it falls to the server to create poaching opportunities with the quality of and the spin on his serve. A heavy slice up the middle to the ad court might well produce an opportunity for the terminator. A topspin serve up the middle to the deuce court often generates a weak return. The goal is for both teammates to participate in holding serve.

## Poaching Checklist

- ☐ Great poachers make winning the service game easy for the server.
- ☐ The key to good poaching skills is knowing which balls to play and which to leave.
- ☐ Know which targets to aim for. "Short to short" devastates the opposition.
- ☐ As terminator, make sure to follow your poach and end up in front of the ball.
- ☐ Make sure the server, or backup, understands how crucial he is to the overall success of your poaching team.
- ☐ Use signals to confuse your opponents, but back the signals up with excellent volleying skills.
- ☐ Do not use signals if you prefer to preserve the spontaneity of the move. Know the trade-off, though—hesitant poachers will remain just that.
- ☐ Remember that half of the value of poaching is to intimidate the receiver.

# 6

# Keeping Control of the Net

..................................

*Excellence is achieved. It is not stumbled upon*
*in the course of amusing oneself. It is built upon discipline*
*and tenacity of purpose.*

..................................

**Racquet Quarterly Magazine**

Controlling the net when your opponents are equally as intent upon doing so is a function of your superior volleying skills and your ability to recognize court-position mistakes by those across the net from you. If the receiver returns your serve with a bruising, wide return into your alley, but makes the mistake of following his ball rather than using the netstrap as he dashes headlong to the net, your angle volley should wrong-foot him and win the point (see chapter three, diagram one). If the server omits his split-stop and charges the net, not stopping until his nose is hanging over it, you know that your lob volley will result in the always-devastating crosscourt lob for a winner. If the opposing terminator neglects his mirroring responsibilities, he may have opened his alley or the middle for your volleys. While some of these responses require that you read and adjust quickly, it is actually easier to keep control of the net against other volleyers than it is to cope with the dreaded lob queens.

I feel very sorry for some of my students because, if I am to believe what they tell me, they are never the recipients of short lobs. It appears that all lob queens reserve their deepest and finest for these poor students, and each time they come off the court, they unfailingly assure me that every single lob their opponents hit definitely bounced *on* the baseline. And, of course, anytime the ball bounces behind you on the court, you must relinquish the net and play defense. Matches can be won by defending the court from behind the baseline, or by playing "one up, one back," for that matter. But neither of these formations can make a dent in the armor of a team possessing superior volleying skills whose expertise extends to maintaining control of the net and not losing it in the face of a barrage of lobs. The only way to establish a pattern of consistent success in doubles is to learn to take the net immediately on every point and keep it by not allowing lobs to bounce behind you.

## HANDLING THE DREADED SERVICE RETURN LOB

In the "California Doubles" staggered formation, all lobs belong to the crosscourt player—in this case the server. However, chasing ten lobs that bounce behind your terminator gets old in a hurry. The following are the three ways to negate the service return lob.

### Assign It to the Terminator

The easiest and simplest way to deter the service return lob is to position the terminator on the service line, hoping to force a crosscourt return instead of a lob. However, stay aware that using this strategy opens the middle of the court, as well as the terminator's alley, for a potential return. If the receiver doesn't notice the potential for a down-the-line return or a sharp drive up the middle, so much the better. If he does, then the terminator has one more option. Instead of moving forward on the sound of his partner's serve, he moves back to handle the lob as an overhead smash. The depth of the lob determines how far back the terminator must move. Either of these options may be very effective for those times when you and your partner have that prickly little feeling that the next service return will definitely be a lob. If your terminator has just made two successful poaches, what will the receiver do next? Lob, of course.

## Australian Formation

When you *think* the returner may be contemplating a lob but you aren't sure, an excellent way to prevent the potential lob from bouncing is the use of the Australian serving formation (see chapter eight for other uses; see also diagram twenty-nine). Because the terminator has moved to his server's side of the court and backed into the crosscourt position, the crosscourt lob is not possible. The server will approach the net on the receiver's side of the court, so if the lob is still headed in a straight line, the server will simply handle it as a volley on his way to the net. Note that using this formation reverses jobs. The terminator is now the crosscourt player, and the server, who has served from the "T," assumes the job of the terminator, playing all of his volleys in a straight line. Using this formation absolutely prevents the service return lob from bouncing.

## Automatic Switch

Some teams prefer the automatic switch to the Australian formation. This plan is exactly like a signaled poach, but it is used when a lob service return is presumed to be in the offing (see chapter five). Although the terminator must be alert for a poach as he is crossing the net, he is actually moving out of the way. The serving partner crosses behind the terminator and takes the lob as a high volley on his way to the net (see diagram nineteen). This, too, changes the jobs. The server becomes the terminator as his partner backs into crosscourt.

The good news is that not all service return lobs are perfect, and some can be handled by the server in the air without needing these alternate strate-

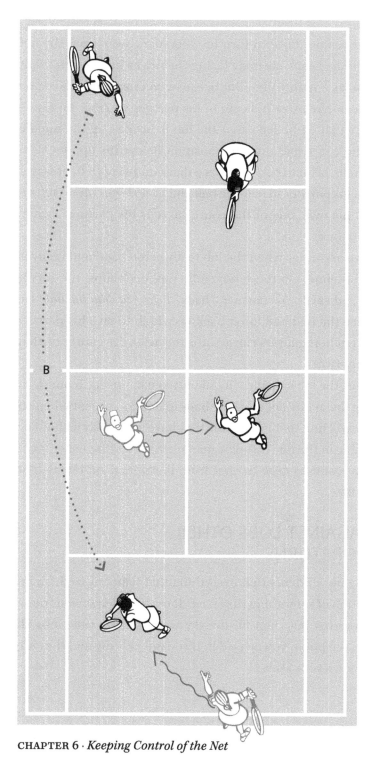

**Diagram 19**

## Playing the Lobbed Return Out of the Air by Using a Signature Poach

As a prearranged plan, you, the server's partner, have moved across the net. Although you remain alert for a poach, you are really moving out of the way so your serving partner can reverse direction and play the service return lob as a high volley on his way to the net.

B

gies. If the server does not have to turn his shoulders away from the net to play the ball, and he keeps his body facing the net as he plays the shot, he can take the lob as a high volley. But because, as crosscourt player, he is captain of the team, he must indicate to his partner whether he wants him to "stay" or "switch." If he feels that the lob is headed up the middle of the court and he can regain his own position before his opponent returns the ball, he tells his partner "stay" (see diagram twenty). If, however, he is pulled behind his partner to play the ball and he feels he cannot return quickly enough to his own side of the court, he tells his partner "switch" (see diagram twenty-one).

Of course, there are times when the lob really is too good and really is bouncing on the baseline. On these hopefully rare occasions, the server should acquiesce and say to his partner, "back," *before he hits the ball*. He should then bounce the ball and lob it back very high to give his partner time to retreat so that both players can assume the defensive court position (see diagram twenty-two).

Most of the time, the lob can and should be taken in the air. Teams that commit to keeping the net by not allowing balls to bounce, except when absolutely necessary, will find that many balls they have previously let bounce are perfectly playable in the air. This play management distinguishes great doubles teams that want to *keep* the net from inexperienced teams that tend to panic and flee.

## DEFENDING AGAINST LOBS OTHER THAN SERVICE RETURNS

I am fond of telling my students that everything that happens to them on the court is a function of something they have done. If the lob queens don't lob their service returns but then fill the sky with unretrievable lobs all through the rest of the point, you caused it. If you are panting and they are sipping mint juleps, it's your fault.

88

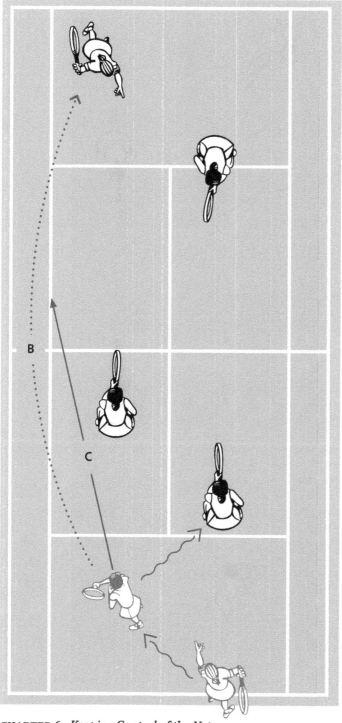

## Diagram 20
## Covering the Service Return Lob Up the Middle

The server has taken the lob in the air from behind his parter. He has issued the command: "Stay!" to the net player, and he will recover to his own side of the court as soon as he has executed his backhand volley off the lob.

B

C

## Diagram 21
### Covering the Service Return Lob Over Your Partner's Head

The terminator has heeded his server's command to switch. The server must play the ball in front of his terminator so that each retains his crosscourt and terminator job.

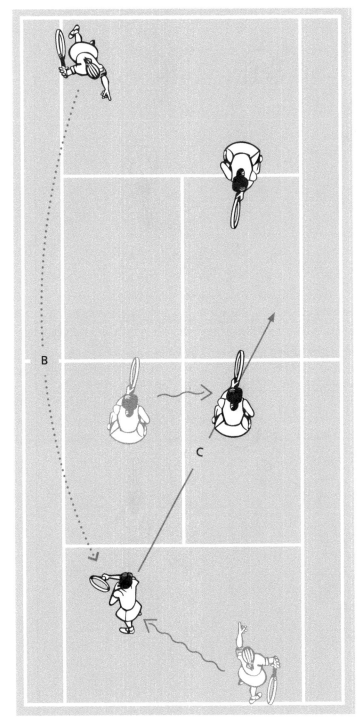

*The Art of Doubles*

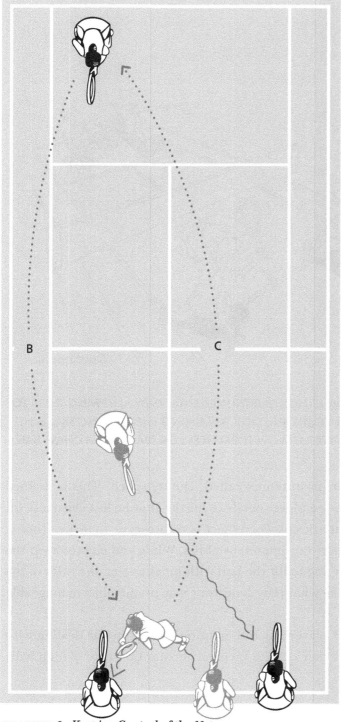

## Diagram 22
## When to Bounce the Lob

If the lob is simply too deep to be played effectively in the air and the server cannot gain his net position before the ball is returned by the opponent, he issues the command "Back!" to the net player, bounces the ball, and both players assume the defensive court position.

B

C

DON'T ACCOMODATE THOSE IRRITATING LOBBERS BY ALLOWING THEM TO OPERATE IN THEIR COMFORT ZONE, RETAINING THEIR TIMING SPACE. HIT DEEP ENOUGH TO PUT THEM ON THEIR HEELS OR MAKE THEM CHASE BALLS.

There is a concept in tennis called "timing space." This is defined as the *room* and *time* a player needs to hit the shot he has chosen to hit (see diagram twenty-three). The object is to preserve your own timing space while robbing your opponent of his. While you cannot keep the lob queens from trying to lift the ball without changing the rules of the game, you *can* make what they send your way predictable, manageable, and ineffective.

The crosscourt player has the main responsibility for dealing with the lobbers. When your team is facing a constant barrage of high balls,

*The Art of Doubles*

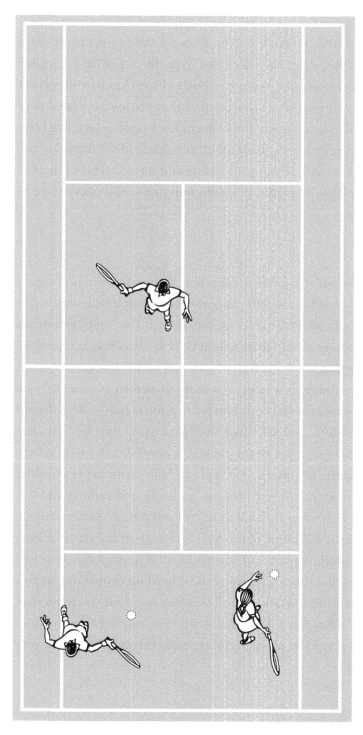

## Diagram 23
## The Value of Timing Space

The player in the deuce court has his timing space. He has the room and time he needs to execute any shot he chooses. The player in the ad court is on his heels. He has neither the room nor the time to choose his shot. Therefore, whether intentionally or not, his ball will rise as it clears the net.

the terminator has little to do, but if he *does* get the opportunity to hit a ball, he should either drop his volley just over the net or hit an angled overhead. If the crosscourt player continuously hits midcourt volleys that bounce on the service line or service returns that are low and land near the baseline, the lob queens are in lob heaven. They have been given their timing space, and they can stand still with one hand in their pockets as they direct perfect missiles over your heads and onto the baseline. But if the crosscourt player's arsenal is good enough, he can prevent all of this from happening.

## Ugly Volleys

Lobbers cannot fire off the perfect deep ball if they have to start their racquet work from shoulder height. Nobody can. Great lobs must be generated from below the waist for leverage and depth. The "ugly" volley has enough loft on it to bounce shoulder height near the baseline and prevent the lobber from hitting anything but a weak ball off his back foot, which the crosscourt player should be able to handle as an easy overhead. I call these volleys uglies because the common perception is that volleys should always be crisp and low, and yet those volleys are the ones lobbers love. "Uglies" rob baseliners of their timing space. Essentially, the ugly return amounts to lobbing the lob queen. The ball will bounce up to his shoulder and, like the ugly volley, will put him on his heels and remove his timing space. Several years ago I watched one of my senior teams struggle against a very proficient lobbing team. My players spent the entire match hitting their shots hard, harder, and hardest in total frustration. They lost badly. After I counseled them, and we worked hard on dropshots and uglies, my team played them again. It is absolutely true that my team won that match 6-0, 6-1. Playing without hubris is difficult, but it really does work. Uglies are executed by using a slightly open racquet face and a very long follow-through.

*The Art of Doubles*

## Angle Volleys

If the crosscourt player angles his volleys short and into the alley in front of the lobber, instead of hitting the ball right back to him, the lobber has again lost his timing space. He may have the *room* to hit a lob, although lobbing is difficult when running full tilt forward, but he certainly will not arrive in *time* to hit a good lob. Careening off balance toward the net is just the way good doubles teams like to see the lob queens reacting to a great angle volley.

## Intelligent Service Returns

Of course, the temptation in the face of people stubbornly trying to remove you from the net is to hit your service return as hard as you can with an "I'll show you" attitude. Unfortunately, the harder you hit it, the easier it is to lob it. The best and most satisfying service return against these players is a lovely dropshot. You might be amazed at the number of times they will simply concede you the point without making any effort to chase it down (see chapter four for an explanation of technique). Sometimes the serve is too hard or too wide to hit a good dropshot because you need time to execute it properly, and you have to be set, body over your feet. If you can't drop the serve, hit an ugly return.

## Fade and Close

If you are using all of these tools and are still struggling with that ball sailing over the terminator's head into the back corner, try "fade and close." This is actually a midpoint role reversal that should surprise the lobber. If you are the serving team and the lob isn't coming off the service return but rather off the crosscourt player's first volley, wait until the lobber hits his *second* shot. At that precise moment, the terminator drifts back to hit an overhead while the crosscourt player closes in to the middle of the court. This can be effective against those queens who prefer lobbing later in the point after they are sure you are both at the net. It can be used just as efficiently if you are the receiving team. The key is to make sure you *wait until the lobber hits his second ball before moving.* The receiver's partner fakes moving forward but does not. The server plays his first volley crosscourt, as usual. Just as the lobber is about to strike ball two, the receiver's partner turns and runs for an overhead as the server closes into the net. Of course, this strategy leaves your team, regardless of whether you are serving or receiving, vulnerable to a crosscourt lob because you have reversed roles, but it often catches the lobbing opponent off guard and produces a winning overhead.

In spite of all of these strategies, it is still truly difficult to compete successfully against people whose sworn mission in life is to keep you off the net. Your shirts will be much wetter than theirs, and a 6-2, 6-2 match might take three hours. You need to remain committed to your plans and understand that beating these lobbers involves, in addition to everything else, a lot of racquet reading and footwork. Both the crosscourt player and the terminator will find themselves drifting back for overheads and immediately scurrying back to their volley positions. At some point in the match, both of you may decide that this is not about tennis anymore; it is just about mental gymnastics and survival. Some lobbers are just so good at what they do that your best "ugly" volleys and dropshots will not thwart them. But if you try to remember that the goal is to play the match in front of you and not behind you, and if you avoid hitting balls that make them salivate, you should be able to control most of these nightmare matches. Above all, recognize that it takes a very different set of plans to beat these lob queens. You play the hand you are dealt. You may wish for three aces and only have a pair of twos. You can't throw in the hand and ask for different cards, nor can you leave the court and request a different set of opponents.

## Net Control Checklist

- ☐ Remember that every time a ball bounces behind you, you must relinquish the net.
- ☐ Service return lobs can be covered in such a variety of ways that they should rarely bounce.
- ☐ Remember your flash cards as the crosscourt player: "stay," "switch," or "back."
- ☐ Take away the lob queens' timing space.
- ☐ Use "ugly" volleys to keep midpoint lobs manageable.
- ☐ Use dropshots and angle volleys to make lob queens miserable.
- ☐ Consider using "fade and close."
- ☐ Make a firm commitment with your teammate to play the ball in the air whenever possible to preserve your offensive court position and maintain net control.

# 7

# Understanding Your
# Jobs on the Court

...............................

*Life always gets harder toward the summit—
the cold increases, the responsibility increases.*

...............................

*Friedrich Nietzsche*

I have been convinced for some time now that a fair number of the "watchers" and "wonderers" believe that certain court positions are more desirable than others because they afford a player a chance to rest or, even better, hide. Timid players feel that they are absolved from the responsibility of actually hitting a tennis ball when occupying one of these "static" court positions, those of the server's partner and the receiver's partner. Some of my bravest students have come forward to confess that my long-held suspicions are indeed accurate. They plead guilty to chanting, "Please, God, don't let the ball come to me," often enough that I fear it becomes some players' mantra— a creed not destined to inspire great teamwork.

On the contrary, great doubles players know that these two court positions are more dynamic than those of server and receiver. They are keenly aware that what a player in one of these court positions does, or does not do, will determine the outcome of a point far more often than what the server or receiver does.

## CONSIDER YOURSELF "ON THE JOB"

Many players have developed attitudes reminiscent of Herman Melville's fictional character, Bartleby the Scrivener, about court positions. Faced with the prospect of having to perform duties they consider hazardous to their mental health, they, like Bartleby, simply dig in their heels and announce that they "would prefer not to." For this reason, I have described those actions of superior doubles players' "jobs" on the court in the hope of persuading doubters and "fearful Freddies" that compliance is an essential ingredient of success.

One aspect of a great doubles team is each player's ability to hit shots in consideration of his partner's job. If one player on a team keeps playing an entire point, something is very wrong. The great doubles player knows not only his own job, but that of his partner, and therefore unselfishly hits the shot that will enable his partner to enter the point and properly do his job without fear of failure or reprisal. Thus, if I serve down the middle, I know I need not cover the return coming through the center because my terminator, honoring his mirroring responsibility, will position himself directly opposite the place where the ball has landed.

The following "job descriptions" will help you understand the individual responsibilities a player has when occupying each of the four roles on the court. When both players execute their respective duties properly, the result is the choreographed smoothness and grace of true teamwork.

## THE SERVER

Hold serve is the first rule of good tennis, singles or doubles. In singles it's all up to you, but in doubles you should get a great deal of help from your partner. However, it is ultimately your responsibility to win your service game. Remember that if you lose it, your opponents don't feel that they broke the *team*. They know that they broke *you*. Only one name is ever attached to a service break. To hold serve, keep these things in mind:

- Get your first serve in. Find a nice, consistent serve that is about 75 percent of the pace you have available to you. Your partner needs a rhythm to poach effectively, and nothing is so discouraging to that eager poacher as a string of false starts on your missed first serves.

- Approach the net and split-stop when your serve hits the court (see chapter nine for a definition of the split-stop). Always assume a neutral position, about halfway between the center line and the alley, no matter where you serve. You must have a decent play on the low, wide returns, the lob, and the center ball if you have served wide. Remember that if you serve wide, your terminator's primary responsibility is the alley. If you serve down the center, your partner will take the return coming straight back through the center, though you must not expect his help on low or hard balls angling away from him. Recognize that if you serve down the center, you and your partner have 80 percent of the court covered, leaving only your partner's alley unprotected (see diagram twenty-four). If you serve wide, you only have about 20 percent of the court well covered (see diagram twenty-five).

- Don't be a "watcher" or a "wonderer" who insists upon serving "wide" to the ad court, assuming you have served "to the backhand." I have never understood this because it makes so many false assumptions. First, it assumes the world is right-handed. Second, it assumes the backhand is weaker. And third, it assumes it is okay to leave 80 percent of the court unprotected. Naturally, none of these assumptions are reasonable. In particular, covering only 20 percent of the court exerts little pressure on your opponent to be accurate.

- Believe that any service return over the net (except, perhaps, the lob in certain circumstances)—anywhere in the court—is yours. Be delighted if your partner intercepts it for you. Even though you may know the information intellectually, it is difficult for the muscles to remember that your partner, at

*The Art of Doubles*

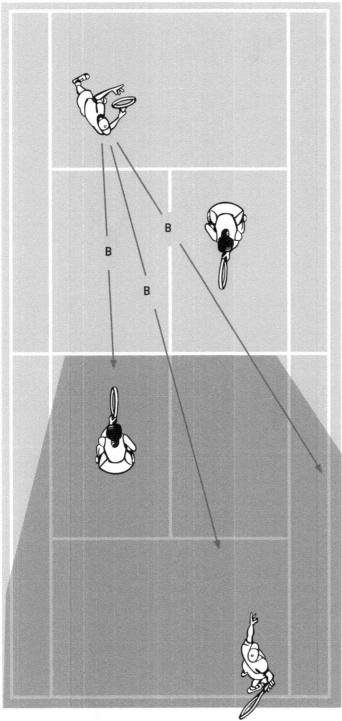

**Diagram 24**

## Serving Down the Middle

Serving down the middle allows a team to protect about 80 percent of its court.

## Diagram 25
## Serving Wide

Serving wide divides a team's responsibilities and allows a receiver to hit into a great deal of unprotected court.

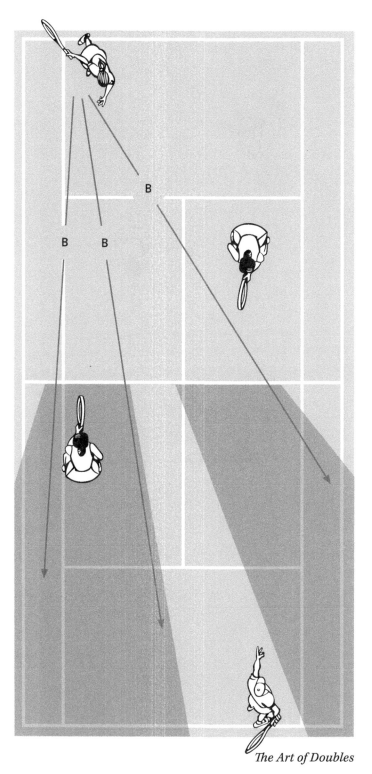

*The Art of Doubles*

the net, *may* begin to move across the net, but may retreat, choosing not to play hard-hit balls angling away, low balls, or even some high balls hit hard enough that he has insufficient time to react. Never relax your racquet. Get your first serve in and hope your partner can put the ball away for you, but don't expect it. Be prepared to hit all balls, never allowing yourself to be distracted by your eager net player's movement.

- Never hurry your first volley. Take care to hit a good, low crosscourt on a wide service return, and a solid reply up the middle on a return aimed up the middle. Remember that if the ball bounces on your side of the net, it bounces. Half-volleys are perfectly acceptable. There is no value in rushing your volley to prevent a ball from bouncing when prudence would dictate a half-volley.

Above all, remember that it is not your job to put the ball away. You are the crosscourt player and thus the worker bee. You set the ball up, and your terminator gets the glory and the applause.

## THE SERVER'S PARTNER

In the position of server's partner, you have many responsibilities. This is not a time to rest and pray that the ball doesn't come to you. This is a time to play an active role in winning the service game. Imagine the following scenario:

Server places a first serve down the middle. Partner, who is afraid to poach, fails to even cover the middle. Service return is hit up the middle and falls good, un-played. 0-15. Server serves an excellent serve (which he has communicated in advance to his partner) wide to the backhand of the player in the ad court. The receiver can do nothing but play a weak lob barely over the head of the net player. The net player says nothing and simply sashays to his ad court, remaining at the net and assuming the server will hit the ball. Server is caught unaware and has no play on the ball. 0-30. Server again serves a first serve down the middle. Terminator, embarrassed and determined to avenge all previous wrongs, darts across the court only to poach a ball much too low for a successful attempt and, alas, places the ball in the bottom of the net. 0-40. Server, slightly unhinged and definitely feeling ragged around the edges, double faults. Game. Server's partner, if, in fact, he is still wanted as a member of this team, needs education.

As the server's partner, always keep these points in mind:

- Your mirroring responsibilities take first priority. Carefully assess whether the serve is being played as an inside or outside ball and adjust accordingly. If it is a wide serve, protect the alley; if it is down the middle, move to the center (see chapter five).

- Remember that the height of a ball changes your targets. Don't try to change the angle of a low ball; return it in the same direction and do so "short to deep." If it is high enough for you to hit down on the ball effectively, return it to a target in the "short to short" direction.

- Distract the receiver and make him hit the shot *you* want him to play, not the shot that *he* wants to play. Draw the ball down your line by faking to the middle; invite an overhead by crowding the net; encourage a cross-court by hugging your alley, and then poach it off if it is a wounded duck— a floater with no pace on it. The more aggressive and fearless you are, the more frozen in fear the receiver becomes.

- Call "out" balls for your team because it is much more difficult for the on-coming server to determine if he might be about to play an "out" ball.

- Be assertive and call the play. Don't be afraid to suggest a service placement that you feel will elicit a predictable response or to ask for that wide serve so that you can execute your fake and tease the receiver into trying your alley. If your server is having trouble volleying that great low, wide crosscourt, it is your job to prompt him to try the Australian formation (see page 119 for an in-depth discussion of this formation).

- Never forget that the most important job for the terminator is to keep the court closed. If you lose heart and begin to get a case of "baseline creep," you are ever-widening the amount of court coverage for the crosscourt player. It is more important to hold your position than it is to be a fearless poacher.

View this court position as one that will earn some free or easy points if you successfully draw the receiver's attention away from the ball toward you. Be a bothersome distraction.

Remember that movement and courage are the keys to playing this court position correctly. More service games are lost because of this player's inactivity than are ever lost by his activity.

## THE RECEIVER

If you don't return serve, there is no service break, and if you don't break serve, you don't win matches. Returning serve successfully requires concentration, thoughtful planning, and careful execution. The receiver should remember these important points:

- Heroes need not apply. Be consistent, not flashy, and remember to hit shots in consideration of your partner's duties. You, like the server, are the worker bee, and your service return should not be a flashy potential winner, but rather the vehicle that enables your terminator to enter the point. However, to avoid becoming too predictable, sprinkle in a fair number of offensive lobs and an occasional passing shot down the line or through the middle.

- In general, stick to the shot that allows your partner to enter the point—the low, wide crosscourt that lands no deeper than the service line. A deep service return in doubles is a poor choice unless you can give assurances that you can hit the back of the baseline and ruin the server's timing space. If the server rushes the net, the deep return is higher and easier to volley. If the server stays back, your "deep" return, which probably lands two to three feet inside the baseline, is right in his comfort zone. Sadly for you, he doesn't even have to move his feet to pass you, or worse yet, lob you on his next shot. Conversely, the low, wide service return is, as we all know, much more difficult to volley, and much more difficult for the baseline-hugger to reach.

- Plan the return in advance, realizing that if the serve is good enough to create an "emergency," that is, the planned return is no longer possible because of the speed, spin, or placement of the serve, a defensive lob is the appropriate response. Players whose strength is their return of serve always know when they are having an emergency and do not foolishly stick to a plan that is no longer an option for those conditions. They do not allow themselves to get too ambitious for the situation. If they can get their racquets on a ball, they put that ball in play using the defensive lob whenever necessary.

- Don't be a "watcher" or a "wonderer." Don't stand around admiring your return. Never indulge in the "between-point" luxuries of awe and admiration, no matter how well you have played the return. Always expect the furry little yellow thing to come back one more time. Follow your return to the net, bearing in mind that the placement of your service return starts your netstrap responsibility (see chapter three, diagram one). Even if the serve pulls you wide, it is your responsibility to play a return that will not put your team in jeopardy. Hot-dogging is not percentage tennis. Dirty looks at your partner are not permitted. He will enter the point and help you when possible, but remember, he will not intercept low balls angling away from him.

- Be prepared to play all balls, as the server must be, and be pleasantly surprised when help is provided.

- Your primary goal is to make your terminator the hero.

*The Art of Doubles*

# THE RECEIVER'S PARTNER

Whether or not your team breaks serve is largely dependent on what this player does, or doesn't do, in this court position, just as whether a service game is held depends largely upon what the server's partner does, or doesn't do. The receiver's partner is the dynamic counterpart to the server's partner. The receiver's partner should keep the following in mind:

- Protect against a poach from the server's partner. Because your eyes are riveted to the server's partner, you will easily see that player begin a poaching move on your partner's return. Move laterally along your service line, being careful to stay in line with your opponent's racquet. This movement will often allow you to intercept what would otherwise be a putaway poach. Your first duty in this court position is defense. Take it seriously, and if the server's partner poaches, don't be a coward and bail out. Often a stab at the ball can rescue an otherwise lost point.

- Don't be a linesperson, even if your court position begins on the service line. A good player often lets his receiving partner handle the job of calling the serve in or out so he can watch the potential poacher more carefully. (You call your own service line in singles, don't you?)

- Once you have determined that the server's partner is not making a move to poach your partner's return, immediately assess two factors:

  1. Is the server coming to the net behind his serve?
  2. What is the height of your partner's return as it crosses the net?

If the answer to question number one is no, or if the server is midcourt and the ball *bounces* in front of him, allowing time to choose a shot, question number two is irrelevant. Immediately start forward, taking care to mirror the ball correctly. In this scenario, the server is perfectly capable of hitting behind you into your alley (see diagram twenty-six).

If the answer to question number one is yes, then question number two becomes very important because the height of the service return to be volleyed

## Diagram 26
## When Not to Poach: Scenario One

The receiver, in the deuce court foreground, has hit an excellent service return. His partner, in the ad court foreground, is an excellent volleyer, renowned for her poaching skills and is eager to cross and put the ball away on this point. However, she sees that the server is not approaching the net and that her partner's return will bounce in front of that server. Because the server can easily aim a ball into his alley, prudence dictates that the eager poacher honor her mirroring responsibilities and wait for a better opportunity.

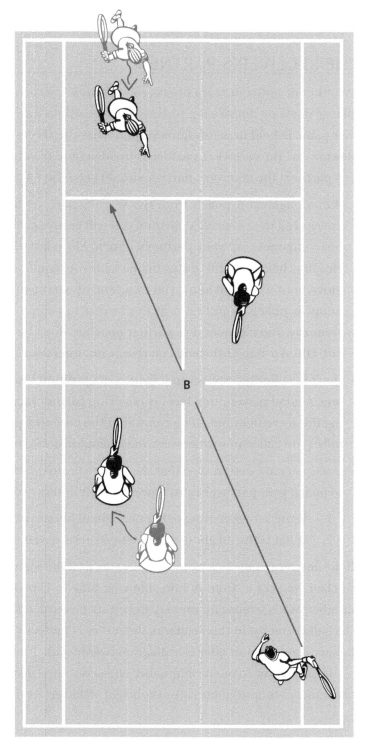

B

*The Art of Doubles*

by the server determines where you must go next. If the return is high enough to allow the server to volley behind you into your alley, you must immediately attempt to mirror the ball and hope to fend off a ball aimed at you (see diagram twenty-seven). This move is critical and yet often neglected by "watchers" and "wonderers" who are sloppy about their court positions. When this court position adjustment is made, the server is forced either to hit crosscourt accurately or pay for allowing his ball to wander toward the person closer to the net—a regrettable "deep to short" error for which you should immediately make him pay. Failure to recognize the need to mirror and move forward, even though the return is high, allows the server to play his shot *anywhere* in the court and be confident that he is hitting "deep to deep."

If the answer to question number one is yes, and the answer to question number two is "low enough to make the server's first volley difficult," *no matter how wide*, then your wonderful partner has set the stage for you to make one of the most satisfying moves of great doubles. If the server is faced with volleying a low ball off his shoe tops, you know that it will be difficult, if not impossible, for him to change its angle and hit behind you. You are free to move toward the center and be prepared to poach off his weak volley. When you move, you will not know how low his volley will be when it crosses the net. It may even pop over your head. It may even be too wide to reach, but you *do* know that if it is to clear the net at all, it will come back at the same angle your partner created with his splendid return. Now is not the time for hesitation or timidity. Be aggressive! This move is one of the great "one-two punch" combinations in doubles (see diagram twenty-eight). Your partner hits a great return; you step in and terminate the point with a forcing volley. Never worry about "false moves." Retreat if the ball is too low to make a decent volley. As noted previously, it is possible that the ball might even pop over your head. Remember that your partner is always alert to play *all* balls and will back you up. This move is the counterpart to the server's partner's poach and is as distracting and upsetting to the server as the poach is to the receiver. And it is barrels of fun.

## Diagram 27
### When Not to Poach: Scenario Two

The mad poacher is eager to try again. This time her eyes light up as she sees the server approaching the net, but alas, she suddenly sees that her partner has hit a very ugly return which has clearerd the net by a good five feet. If she begins a poach, the server can easily volley into her alley because the ball is so high. Again the patient poacher must cover her alley and await another opportunity.

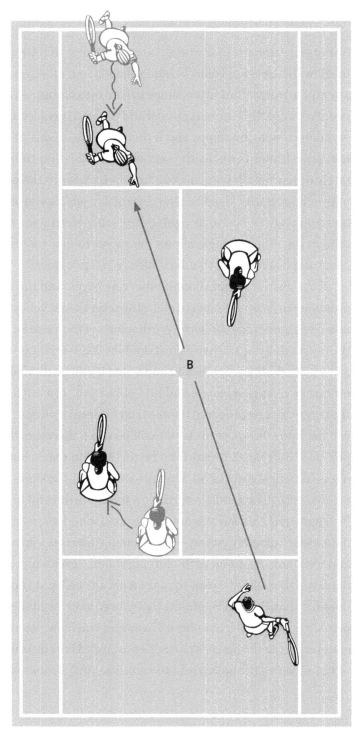

*The Art of Doubles*

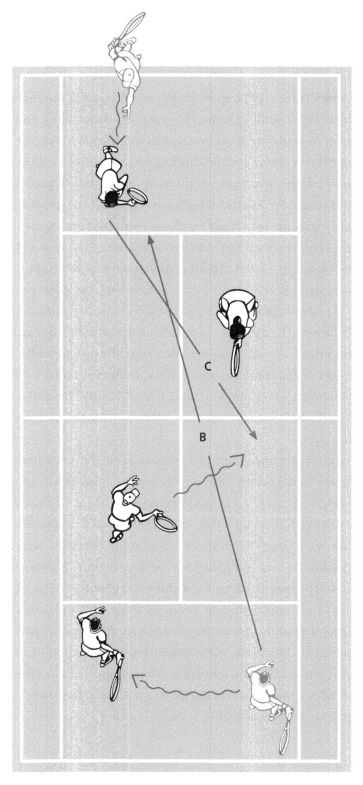

## Diagram 28
### When to Poach

The passionate poacher is rewarded. His deuce court partner hits a wonderfully low return. The server is approching the net and will be faced with a volley he must dig out of his shoe tops. It would be virtually impossible for the server to volley this ball into his alley, so the poacher is free to romp across the net and poach the "wounded duck."

The receiver's partner is the most important job on the court. It requires an assessment of the server's ability, the server's partner's movement, and your returning partner's expertise on every single point you play this position. If the server is a wily veteran, capable of hitting low and angled volleys off his shoelaces, you probably won't get too many opportunities to poach. And yet before you even consider whether an offensive move is even possible, you must play defense, watching carefully for the server's partner's poach. His opportunity comes before yours. You must, in each game, if not on every serve, determine your partner's ability to hit a good, offensive crosscourt for you. Your movement is predicated on this assessment because you *must wait at the "T" if you are going to intercept the server's volley.* You can't automatically move forward to mirror (a common error) and then decide, "Oops, I think I better cross," because you have dramatically increased the angle you have to travel. If you think you might have a chance to poach off the server's volley, you *must* be patient and wait at the "T" until his ball *is in the air.* If it is the right ball to move on, you will have time to catch up to it and hit a forcing volley.

Each job on the court is very important, and on each side of the net, proper execution of the starters' jobs—server and receiver—must occur before the jobs of the finishers, the server's and receiver's partners, may begin. Certainly, no job is a place for resting. Never catch yourself becoming an orange cone, standing around and buying tickets to the event unfolding on the court. Starters have the responsibility for beginning the point to their team's advantage. Finishers have the added pressure of deciding if and when to enter the point, and there is very little time to make that decision. Yet those decisions often determine the outcome of a point, a game, or even a match. The ability to play these dynamic finishing roles properly and confidently is the culmination of those skills mentioned earlier:covering the center, having superior poaching skills, playing good defense, taking care of the lob when it is assigned to you, and knowing your proper mirroring duties.

Playing great doubles requires that you see and understand all the tiles in a complicated mosaic. One tile may be beautiful, but meaningless, and yet when each tile is fitted into its proper place, the result is a work of art best viewed by stepping away and appreciating the larger picture.

The great doubles machine functions at a very high level of expertise, forged out of each player being in the right place, taking the right ball, saying the right thing, executing jobs well, and playing with a partner you trust and respect.

## Jobs Checklist

- ☐ Don't expect to hide or rest in good doubles. Each of the four court positions is a highly visible and demanding job.
- ☐ Your doubles team will achieve its best results when both players enter the majority of the points, achieving a rhythm and balance to the action.
- ☐ Servers and receivers have the responsibility for starting the point to the team's advantage. They are the "worker bees."
- ☐ Service games are often won solely by the aggressive play of the server's partner.
- ☐ Service games are often broken by the dynamic intervention of the receiver's partner into the point.
- ☐ In good doubles, it is particularly true that the whole is greater than the sum of its two parts.

# 8

# Flexibility: A Powerful Weapon

......................................

*... lucidity of thought ... freedom from prejudice and freedom from stiffness, openness of mind ... all these seem to go along with a certain happy flexibility of nature, and to depend upon it.*

......................................

*Matthew Arnold*

Imagine playing a match like this one: The score is close, but your team sees the chance to seize some momentum. Suddenly, you, as terminator, are presented with an easy, poachable ball, so you swiftly cross and play the shot to a target, only to watch one of your opponents dive for the ball, close his eyes, recoil, gasp, and hit it off his frame for a clean winner over both of your heads. As you stand there in shocked silence, he apologizes. You think nothing of it until three points later, he does it again. Another apology ensues, this time accompanied by a shoulder shrug. You raise your eyebrows, but your partner tells you not to worry. He can't possibly do it again. You continue to play your balls to his side of the court whenever possible because he is a gasping, lucky, incompetent idiot. Two and a half sets later, not only is he still doing it, but he also manages to win the match on a desperate stab accompanied by a particularly savage groan followed by a sheepish grin.

This guy is probably still doing it on somebody else's court to some equally unbelieving and inflexible opponents. So why don't you change your strategy or hit a different shot?

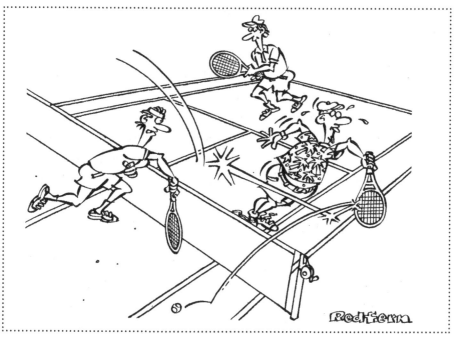

WHEN YOUR STUMBLING OPPONENT CONTINUES TO SOMEHOW
RETURN YOUR PUTAWAYS, BE FLEXIBLE ENOUGH TO CHANGE THE
SELECTION OF YOUR SHOT.

## FLEXIBILITY REQUIRES CONFIDENCE

Stubbornness, hubris, and inflexibility are all weaknesses of the "watcher"
and "wonderer" teams. The ability to remain flexible in a trying situation,
such as the one just mentioned, takes great confidence, both in yourself
and in your partner. When you are winning and things are purring smoothly, flexibility is not a consideration, but it is often the single factor that can
rescue your team from a dire situation. Consider, for example, that if you
win the toss, maybe your team shouldn't *always* opt to serve first. There is
no other time that the server is more likely to lose his serve than the first
game of the match. Nerves haven't quite settled yet, and a steady server

may not yet have found his groove. If you receive first and snatch a quick first game, you will be up a break before you've taken off your jacket.

Flexibility, both as a player and as a team, includes the ability to recognize when your strategy is in error, when a different formation or pace shot might produce better results, and when and how to adjust *quickly*. The definition of insanity is doing the same thing over and over and expecting a different result. At some point, you have to believe that the guy hitting winners off his frame isn't going to stop—at least not on that day. Never wait until you are mired in a mudhole so deep that you make adjustments only to see if the match can be saved. Learn to evaluate each situation and know your options. Use strategic changes to maintain your lead or stay even in a match, not to try to grasp it from a stinging defeat. Your demonstration of flexibility shows your opponents that you have an answer for everything and you will counter each strength they have. The late Arthur Ashe said Jimmy Connors was the greatest player who ever lived because he never lost a match—he just sometimes ran out of time before he could hit upon the winning strategy.

## ASK YOURSELF A COUPLE OF KEY QUESTIONS

Being behind in a match is not a personal reflection of how well you play tennis, nor is it an indictment on your character. It is frequently a temporary problem for which you can find a solution if you stay flexible and calm, but it can escalate quickly into a hopeless situation if you succumb to blind panic.

Anytime the score is not in your favor, regardless of whether you are down one game or six games, the question you and your partner should ask is, "Are they winning, or are we losing?" The answer will help you determine which strategy you should use to reverse the tide.

If you are missing manageable volleys, double-faulting, hitting playable balls out, or failing to return serve, then they are not *winning*, you are *losing*, and the fault is on your side of the net. Making winners doesn't win matches, but making unforced errors definitely loses them.

The other question you should ask is: "Are we changing a winning game strategy?" This error is more thoroughly discussed in chapter eleven, but you and your partner need to evaluate this possibility on the court and decide if that is the reason you are falling behind. If you won the first set by having the terminator stand on the service line to take away the service return lob and you lost the second set because the terminator resumed his net position and you were lobbed to death, well, it's not rocket science.

## How to Eliminate Unforced Errors
## and Regain Your Rhythm

If you determine that the problem *is* the number of unforced errors your team is making, then you must resist the temptation to "hurry and catch up," which will only compound the problem. This is a common pitfall for teams who secretly believe that the people across the net are not really as good as they are. You begin to feel a tinge of embarrassment and hope no one watching realizes that you are down 1-4 to those inferior people across the net. You try to fix it quickly by overplaying balls and trying low-percentage shots, all of which serve to increase the number of unforced errors you make.

If you find yourself down 1-4, and you know that you got there with your own little hatchet, try to be patient. However long it took you to dig yourself into this hole, believe that it will take you twice as long to climb out of it.

Gain composure by playing longer points. Resist the temptation to attempt service aces and service return winners. Settle for service return with too much net clearance, if that is the only way you can get the ball in play. Use more lobs. Take pace off your volleys, even if that means the ball will come back when it shouldn't. The more balls you hit, the more time you will have to settle down and find your rhythm. Give your opponents a chance to make a mistake before you do, and the score should gradually shift in your favor.

## What to Do About Forced Errors

If most of the points you are losing are *forced* errors resulting from your opponents' stellar play, then you must change your tactics. Alter your strategy calmly and perhaps more than once. The process is frequently one of trial and error. Luckily, there is rarely a time clock on a tennis court. If you normally play under those restraints, your adjustments must be made much more quickly. The following information describes a few tactics.

Sometimes, the better you hit the ball, the better it comes back. Instead of stubbornly trying to hit harder and harder, hoping to knock the racquet out of your opponent's hand, it is more prudent to take pace off of your shots, perhaps by using some underspin. If you've ever had an opponent say to you, "Gee, you hit a nice ball," the translation is, "Gee, I love how hard you hit the ball because I never have to do anything but block it." Against those players, it is better to hit softly, forcing them to create their *own* pace, which will then elicit, "Gee, I hate to play against junk," which freely translated reads, "You made me work too hard, and I don't like it." Make sure you analyze your opponents' ability to handle pace or soft balls and be certain that you are not losing because you are feeding them their preference.

If you and your partner execute favorite shots well, but you don't seem to be winning those points, maybe you are too predictable. Being flexible means acknowledging a tactical flaw such as this without getting angry and trying to hit the shot even *better* or harder. If the guy across the net is standing in the way of your cannonball forehand return and knows it's coming, it is probably a good bet that he's going to get it back, which will only encourage you to hit even harder, perhaps this time finding the fence instead of his racquet. Be flexible and pull a different arrow from your quiver, thus setting the stage for the unexpectedness of your favorite shot.

*The Art of Doubles*

## RECOGNIZE YOUR OWN PREDICTABLE STROKES

One stroke that often becomes much too predictable is the serve. A player with a cannon for a serve may win his service game at love the first time he serves. Then he loses a point or two the next time he serves, and soon he wonders why he is losing his serve by the second set. If you allow a good player to see the same ball often enough, he will eventually figure out a way to handle it. Keep receivers off balance by mixing the speed and spin of your serve constantly.

A word of caution: Predictability may be the reason you are losing, but it may also be the reason you are winning. If you have hit the same service return seventeen times in a row, and seventeen times in a row the server has volleyed it into the bottom of the net, don't change it on the off chance that number eighteen *might* come back. Just keep hitting the same old boring winning return. This is tantamount to changing a winning game strategy.

## THE AUSTRALIAN SERVING FORMATION

If you, as the server, have just dumped seventeen straight volleys into the net because that crosscourt service return is too hard to handle, a change in strategy is sixteen muffed volleys overdue. One strategy you should consider using is the Australian serving formation, which is designed to eliminate the receiver's crosscourt return (see diagram twenty-nine).

To set up this formation, first assume you are serving to the deuce court. Move away from your normal position and stand near the center mark, as if you are playing singles. Your partner, who would normally stand in the ad court and face the deuce court receiver, stands in the *deuce* court and faces the deuce court receiver on the diagonal. Your partner's exact position is somewhat flexible, but he must stand near enough to the alley to ensure that the crosscourt return is no longer possible and far enough away from the net to be able to cover the lob over his head. (This formation also takes away the service return

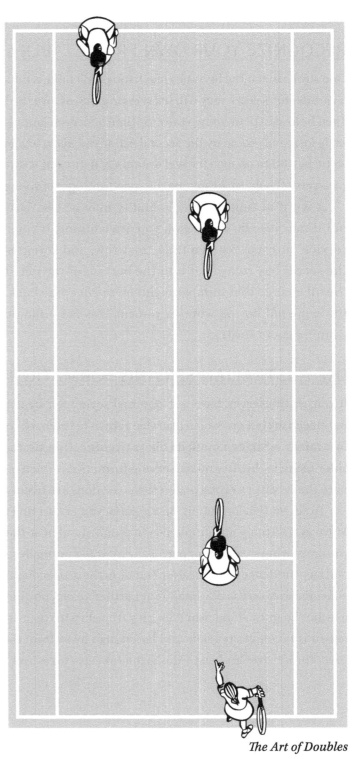

### Diagram 29
## Using the Australian Serving Formation

The players in the near court are in the Australian serving formation. The server is serving from the base line "T." The partner is positioned in the deuce court, back far enough in her box to cover a lob and near enough to her alley to prevent a cross-court service return. The receiver in the far court has adjusted to the server by moving to her left and her partner has repositioned herself very close to the center service line in anticipation of a down-the-line return.

*The Art of Doubles*

lob, as discussed in chapter six). Many teams serve only down the center when using this formation, but this is not a hard rule. No matter where you serve, if the receiver chooses a down-the-line return rather than a lob, he is faced with the difficult task of changing the direction of the ball toward the highest part of the net, near the alley. Using the Australian formation frequently forces an otherwise consistent and "grooved" receiver to lose his rhythm and make unforced errors because he must now play his returns in an unfamiliar direction.

Be sure to practice this formation repeatedly before using it in a match. Because the server comes to the net in the "wrong" direction, it may feel "backwards." The server's partner has *total* responsibility for the crosscourt lob because the server's path to the net takes him away from the angle of the ball. Remember that using this formation reverses your jobs. The server becomes the terminator, making sure to play all balls in front of him, and the receiver's partner stays the crosscourt player.

Use this formation when serving either to the deuce or ad court to prevent receivers from hitting devastating crosscourts or service return lobs, or simply use it occasionally to keep the receiving team off balance. It works well as a surprise tactic in a very long service game when your team needs a quick point.

## THE "I" FORMATION

A variation of the Australian formation is the "I" formation, in which your partner positions himself astride the center service line (see diagram thirty). As the server, you serve from the center mark and should serve down the middle. Your partner assumes a ready position *below* the level of the net or risks getting hit in the head. Since you begin the point in "I" formation, every point is a signaled poach, with its direction indicated by your partner's hand signal, which you should acknowledge verbally. This formation taxes your partner's endurance and both of your concentrations, but it can effectively confuse the receiving team or lure them into watching the poacher's direction rather than the ball.

## Diagram 30
## Using the "I" Serving Formation

The serving team has chosen to use the "I" formation because the team enjoys confusing the opposition with their signaled moves and because the net player crouched in the middle of the court is both agile and an excellent volleyer. Alas, the receiver is a wily old veteran with many years experience. She has taken two steps backward from her normal receiving position in order to give herself additional time before she must strike the ball. After the serve is struck, the net player and server must begin immediately to move in their signaled directions. The reciever will note the poacher's direction and then aim his return away from her, toward the court to be covered by the server. In this manner, the reciever will always beat the potential poacher at the guessing game. To vary her strategy, this smart reciever may choose to smack a return up the middle, hoping to catch both players going in opposite directions midstride.

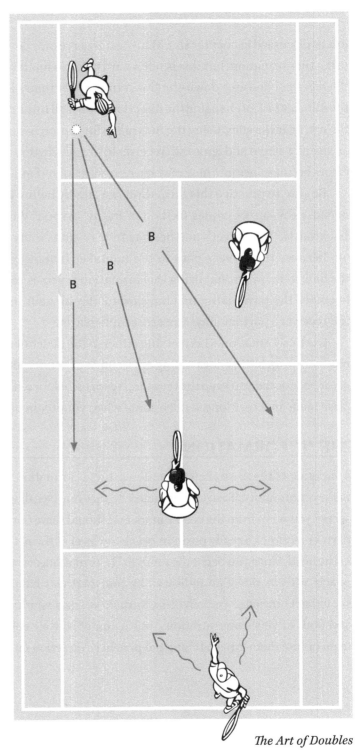

*The Art of Doubles*

# DEFENDING AGAINST THE AUSTRALIAN FORMATION

If the Australian formation is used against you, the receiving team, do not let it rattle you. Quickly adjust your thinking and change your targets. Whether you play the deuce court or the ad court, as soon as you see the server move to the center mark, shift slightly away from your alley and toward the center service line to protect against the down-the-middle ace. Your partner should station himself as near the center service line as he dares, because you can no longer choose to hit a crosscourt groundstroke.

As receiver, you have only two options:

1. A groundstroke or chipped return down the line that changes the direction of the ball and makes you the terminator.
2. A stinging return up the middle of the court.

Every formation has a weakness, and the middle is the weak point in the Australian. There are no other options because the server's partner has the crosscourt lob covered. Trying to invent one is recklessly foolhardy (see diagram thirty-one). If you choose to go down the line with your return, play the ball very early to allow the time you need to get your racquet around and change the direction of the ball.

Your service return will not suffer if you stick to the two high-percentage tennis options described above. Resist the temptation to be a hero and make your opponents pay for doing this to you.

# DEFENDING AGAINST THE "I" FORMATION

If the "I" formation is used against you, don't panic. Take a few steps back from your normal receiving position to give yourself a little more time. Those extra few seconds will let you see the court and your opponents' movements, especially those of a poaching net opponent who, because of your position adjustment, must now move *before* you hit the ball if he is to cover the court adequately (see diagram thirty). Once you note the poaching direction, you

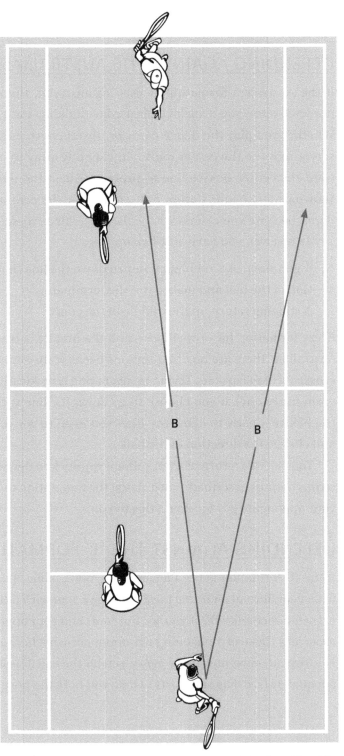

### Diagram 31
## Defending Against the Australian Formation

When receiving against the Australian formation, return either with a down-the-line chip or drive or a down-the-middle drive. No other options exist. Resist the temptation to invent one.

*The Art of Doubles*

can safely return the ball back to the server, either crosscourt or down the line, knowing that the ball will be unmolested by the net player. A return played sharply up the middle is often effective against the "I" formation because your opponents are now going in different directions, and the ball might land untouched between them. Your partner should not crowd the center against this alignment as he would against the Australian or he will block your potential crosscourt. Above all, as with the Australian, don't allow this different formation to confuse or distract you. Remember, your job is to get the ball into play, and using a high, deep lob is never a bad idea.

## HOW TO DEFEND AGAINST A MONSTER SERVE

If one of your opponents owns a monster serve that has given both your team fits throughout the match, and you realize that you must break this serve to stay competitive, try beginning each point of the game with both of you in the defensive court position (see diagram thirty-two). This does several things. First, it gives you more time to return serve because you will play from a stationary position well outside the baseline, as if you were playing singles. (Normally, in doubles you would use a service return as an approach shot.) Don't worry that an errant return could drift too close to the net man; your partner's position behind the baseline effectively eliminates the opponent's poach. Additionally, the opposing server's rhythm may be thrown off just because the court across the net suddenly looks so different to him. His usual targets are gone, and if you can just get that serve into play, he may lose all sense of where to place his first volley. Be careful about your court position, and be patient enough to approach the net on the proper ball (see chapter three on court position).

You may also use this formation as a serving team, but I don't recommend it, because this relinquishes the advantage your team enjoys by starting the point. Anytime your team serves, you control the manner in which the point starts, and you do that with the pressure the server's partner puts on the receiver. A

## Diagram 32
## Returning Serve From the Defensive Court Position

Consider receiving serve from the defensive court position. It gives you the opportunity to take more time with the return, eliminates the worry of a poach, and may make your opponents very angry because it indicates to them that much longer points containing a significant number of lobs are on the horizon.

*The Art of Doubles*

poach is always a threat. Good doubles teams maintain the aggressive posture when serving and, as the receiving team, resort to defense when necessary.

## AN EFFECTIVE TACTIC AGAINST IMPENETRABLE OPPONENTS

If the problem is not an opponent's big serve, but simply your inability to make a dent in a good team's otherwise impenetrable armor, the defensive court position formation can be equally effective. Several years ago, my partner and I were playing an important match against a fine team that was capable of being either average or brilliant. Unfortunately for us, we met them on a brilliant day. We lost the first set 6-0 in what seemed like ten seconds, not because we were making errors, but because they hit winner after winner from impossible places on the court, creating angles that I would have thought were simply not options. At 0-6, we, as the receiving team, decided to begin the set from our defensive court position and did so every time they served. This, to our surprise and delight, upset and enraged them so that we won the match 0-6,6-1,6-0. Most reversals are not that dramatic, but using good defense can boost you back into a match that would otherwise slip away.

## FLEXIBILITY IN THE FACE OF LOB QUEENS

If a match is sliding away from you because you are being lobbed to death, there probably isn't a lot you can do except dig in and be patient. So often in this situation, one or both players on a team will give in. "I'm not doing this anymore. This isn't tennis. It isn't fair. If they want it that badly, they can have it. I'll go play golf." Then your overheads begin to hit the back fence. The way out of this frustrating dilemma is to relax and appreciate your opponents' strategy. Take it as a compliment. They certainly realize that you volley too well for them to pass you, and so they resort to trying your patience and endurance by hitting every ball twenty feet into the air. No one enjoys having to wrestle with the lob queens, but you can prevail if you can be flexible. Stick with your plan and avoid hitting balls into their timing space. Acknowledge that it will not be over quickly, that you will hit many angled overheads, that the ball will come back often, and that this is no time for a temper tantrum. You may win the match 6-2, 6-2, but it may take more than two hours. The satisfaction is worth the effort.

## IN THE END, BE A GRACIOUS LOSER

If you've tried the Australian, used the defensive court position, tried to become less predictable, varied your serves, eliminated your unforced errors, and you still cannot prevail, then be satisfied with a job well done. Don't fall victim to hubris, blaming a loss on bad luck. If you've tried everything, and nothing worked, maybe your opponents *are* better than you are. Maybe they played over their potential, in the "zone," that day. If so, learn from their performance and have the grace to say, "You played great," not "We played badly." A great doubles team can actually make you play badly if their mastery of the game exceeds yours. It is wise to acquire the capacity to appreciate the artistry.

**Flexibility Checklist**

☐ Ask yourselves, as a team, whether an unfavorable score is due to your own errors, your opponents' superior play, or changing a winning game. The answer will help you choose the proper strategy to reverse the momentum.

☐ Be careful not to become too predictable.

☐ Know how to use or defend against Australian and "I" formations.

☐ Never be afraid to offer a good defense to a superior offense.

☐ Use strategy changes to help you win matches, not just to prevent you from losing them.

☐ If you tried everything and you still lost, it should be a peaceful defeat.

*The Art of Doubles*

# 9

# Gaining Command
## of the Intangibles

......................................

*"Mr. Kikady, how do you maintain your concentration, stay re-*
*laxed and maintain accuracy under the pressure of playing for*
*hundreds of thousands of dollars?"*

*"I do not know, but I think, it is not by strength but by art."*

......................................
***Sandy Dunlop,*** The Golfing Bodymind

Great doubles teams make a series of complicated actions look deceptively easy and graceful. Denise McCluggage, writing in *The Centered Skier*, says, "Grace is a warmer word for efficiency." Four centuries ago, the Italian diplomat Baldassare Castiglione introduced the word *sprezzatura* in *The Book of the Courtier*. The English language does not possess a word that conveys all that is meant by this Italian term. It refers to a certain casualness, a grace of movement, even a kind of natural, offhanded manner which, while giving the impression of absolute effortlessness, is actually acquired through tedious hours of practice and strict discipline. Castiglione says further of those who possess *sprezzatura*:

*For it implants in the minds of the spectators the notion that one who so easily does well knows how to do much more than what he is doing, and if he expended study and labor on what he is doing he could do it much better ... Likewise, in dancing a single step, a solitary graceful and effortless movement of the body quickly reveals the proficiency of the dancer.*

When you watch great doubles teammates perform their jobs correctly, you marvel at the ease with which a perfectly placed service return is executed off a very difficult serve. You stare in admiration as the receiver's partner crosses in front of his teammate at precisely the right moment to end the point with his poach. Not only is the skill readily apparent from the actions of the players, but the sense that there are reserves of ability, as yet undisplayed, is also present. Nothing looks difficult or awkward. The harder you train and the more you practice, the easier it is to walk on the court with an air of quiet self-confidence that will be immediately obvious to your opponents and strike terror in their fragile psyches. More importantly, this should translate into better racquet control and shot selection.

If we consider for a moment the opposite of *sprezzatura*—a pair who over-hit their shots, swing at their volleys, go for too much too soon in the point, and neglect touch shots—a picture of a tense and awkward team emerges. Regardless of the score, this team's opponents believe they are never out of the match because implosion and self-destruction are always a distinct possibility. Castiglione says:

*... and on the other hand, to strain and, as they say, "to drag by the hair" ... imparts the greatest awkwardness and causes everything, no matter how ... important, to be held in low esteem.*

Therefore, it is important to remember that a deft "touch" volley does more than just win the point. It sends the message that you are in absolute control of your skills, your shot selection, and the match. Never shout when a whisper is enough. Regardless of the score, your opponents will begin to feel despondent and unable to cope with the depth of your reserves.

As the match progresses and you begin to choose wisely from among the array of shots available to you, you create the impression that what your opponents are witnessing is just the bare beginning of all the possible ways you have to beat them. When an operatic diva hits "E" above high "C" with ease, you are aghast at what reserves she obviously possesses that

*The Art of Doubles*

you haven't yet seen. The important point here is that she never need hit that higher note. You just imagine that she could. When you choose to play a soft dropshot rather than over-hit that big forehand, your opponents are silently screaming, "What next? What next?" And at that point, the mental war is over. You may or may not own a better shot than that one, but you won't need it.

The old cliché "don't do more than you need to" has merit. There are times when it is important to hit the ball as hard as you can safely hit it. But there are times when doing as little as you must to win the point—a soft angle—and then quickly turning your back to the net and walking away makes an absolutely devastating impression on your opponents. You are silently saying to them, "This is easy. I have so many weapons available that I need only pick the smallest one that will get the job done."

It isn't always easy to maintain this kind of grace and composure in a very tight match, but the true practitioner of *sprezzatura* will never seem unnerved. He will toil with ultimate confidence in his skills even on a bad day, and that, in itself, is very much a kind of victory.

It is true that the whole is most definitely greater that the sum of its parts, and when analyzing great doubles teams, certain "intangibles" are common to all of them.

## TIME: THERE NEVER SEEMS TO BE ENOUGH

One of the most frequent complaints I hear from aspiring doubles stars is that there simply isn't enough time to hit a shot correctly and accurately. Therefore, their most frequent error is that they rush every movement, every stroke, every ball they hit. It is not uncommon for inexperienced players to serve, race toward the net as fast as they can, and swing wildly at the ball somewhere along the route in this frantic sprint toward total disaster. They are propelled at full gallop by the absolute conviction that all balls travel at speeds in excess of 200 miles per hour.

By contrast, great players always seem to be in slow motion, never rushed, never hurried, never flustered, for two very good reasons.

• **Reason 1:** To become a master of time, you must develop proper ball-watching skills, but it is simply not true that you should *always* watch the ball.

Poor doubles players will turn around and watch their partners hit the ball, hoping that this will provide some clue to what might happen next. Although average players know better than that, *they* will focus on the ball as it crosses the net going *toward* the opponents to perceive its direction. In addition, both poor and average players watch the ball come off their own strings and follow it with their eyes until it lands across the net, and often longer. Highly skilled players, on the other hand, understand that you must always track the ball as it is coming *toward* you, but *never* watch the ball as it is going *away* from you.

Imagine you are the player striking the ball. You know where you intend to hit it, so you know beforehand which opponent will strike the ball next. The moment the ball leaves your strings, your eyes should move to that player's racquet, never pausing for an instant to follow the flight of your shot. Realize that the ball and your opponent's racquet are going to end up in the same place at the same time.

If your partner is the crosscourt player and he is the one striking the ball, you may reasonably expect the ball to appear in front of you, because that is his job. Yet you must be alert in case he makes an error in direction. If your partner is the terminator, you expect his ball to be played short to short, but he might misplay his shot. Discipline yourself to have, to use John Madden's football expression, "linebacker eyes." This means that while the ball is on your partner's strings, even though you *think* you know where the ball is headed, your eyes should be darting from opponent to opponent and back until you see one of their racquets begin its preparation. That player becomes your opponent, and it is his racquet that you must read and react to.

Proper ball-watching skills will allow you to act on your volleys instead of reacting to the ball at the last second. Good eye control will give you at least two to three more seconds to see what you must do to prepare properly to play your shot and will help you to realize that you need not rush all of your strokes. Again, only watch the ball when it is coming toward you—never when it is traveling away from you.

• **Reason 2:** Highly skilled players have the confidence to take the time they need to execute the shot properly. There is absolutely no substitute for early preparation, but, as I endlessly try to convince my students, there is always more time than you think. The trick is to discipline yourself to understand the natural rhythm of a stroke—the cadence of a free-flowing weight transfer and swing of the racquet—to know the amount of time necessary to execute it smoothly, and to have the confidence that the required amount of time exists for the taking. In *The Sweet Spot in Time*, John Jerome says:

*Most infield errors occur because the fielder starts his play before he catches the ball. This is the tiredest cliché in sports, of course— "Look the ball into your hands," even "Keep your eye on the ball"—but it illuminates a little more territory when it is understood in terms of available time. The good performer simply takes all the time there is for the particular move.*

Great doubles teams are composed of players who do not watch each other hit the ball, but instead keep their eyes focused on opponents' racquets. They will find a way, even in the most heated exchanges at the net, to use every available second to hit a controlled and accurate shot. The issue of time is a very important one in tennis. If you have enough of it, it is your team's greatest ally, and if you give your opponents too much of it, they will always find ways to pick you apart.

Therefore, you must find ways to create more time for your team and take it away from the opposing team. You must give a fluid, graceful, unhurried, and relaxed performance while compelling your opponents to look harried, rushed, and unable to think clearly. Your ability to do so is predicated on your understanding of superior racquet work.

## WHEN TO USE DEPTH, PACE, OR FINESSE

Have you ever watched a doubles team work a point until one opponent is off the court and the other lies prone in an alley, only to blow the easy volley into the middle of the back fence? It happens often and is the result of not choosing the racquet speed sufficient to accomplish the task at hand. Overkill—hitting a ball much too hard when placement to open court is sufficient, and underkill—failure to use pace to push a volley past a well-positioned opponent—are maladies of the inexperienced players.

Three intangibles great doubles teams have mastered are: knowing when to volley with pace, when to place a volley deep in the court, and when to use finesse. *Pace* is a function of the speed of the racquet head through a volley and a function of one's ability to bring the racquet to a sudden stop. It is used in what is commonly referred to as the "punch volley." *Depth* is a function of the distance the racquet travels from contact point forward, that is, the length of the follow-through. *Finesse* is the ability to create touch volleys by softening the grip on the racquet and coddling the ball to create a soft, short volley that carries underspin.

If you are to become an expert in choosing the appropriate racquet speed for the job, you must understand these guidelines:

1. Pace is achieved with short and quick racquet work.
2. Depth is achieved with long and slow racquet work.
3. Finesse is achieved by caressing the ball with a gentle hand.
4. Hitting for both depth and pace will almost always send your ball over the baseline (or the sideline) and out.
5. Using a short, but slow, racquet speed will either send the ball into the bottom of the net or give an opponent too much time to choose his weapon.

*The Art of Doubles*

YOUR OPPONENTS HAVE CALLED 911 AND NEED RESPIRATORS;
DON'T IMPRESS THE CROWD WITH A SMOKING VOLLEY TO TH
BASELINE. GET THE BALL IN AND WIN THE POINT!

6.  Using long and slow raquet work takes away the timing space of an op-
    ponent parked near the baseline.
7.  Reserve short and quick raquet work for those times when the pace on
    your ball must keep an opponent who is in a short-court position from
    having the time to react to your shot.
8.  Remember that the primary target on the court is always the ground
    in front of your opponent, not his racquet. Use long and slow work for
    deep-to-deep volleys and short and quick work for short-to-short volleys.
    Stick with this formula and your opponents will never have enough time
    to pick a shot that can hurt you (see diagram thirty-three).

**Diagram 33**
## Racquet-Speed Guidelines

The player in the near ad court is demonstrating the following guidelines:

A. A short follow-through and slow racquet speed is insufficient for a ball to clear the net.

B. Use a long follow-through and slow racquet speed to send a ball deep to the shoes of a baseline hugger.

C. Trying to hit for both depth and pace, using a long follow-through and fast racquet speed, will send the ball over the baseline.

D. Use a short follow-through and quick racquet speed to punish a ball in the "short to short" direction and thus end the point.

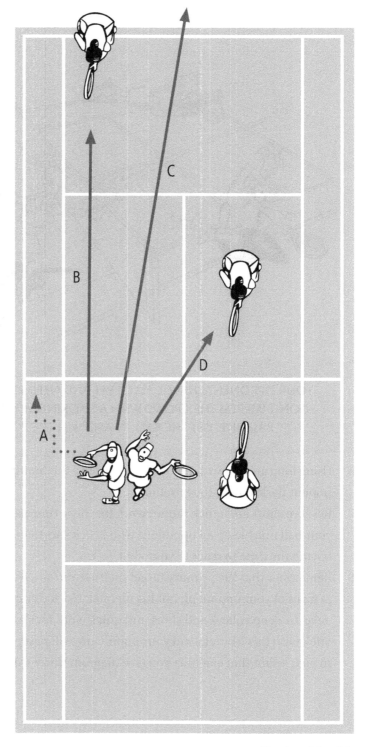

*The Art of Doubles*

## CULTIVATE THE DROP OR UNDERSPIN VOLLEY

Nothing is more frustrating than seeing your opponents hugging the baseline and being unable to play the ball gently enough to have it drop unplayed in front of them. The solution is to cultivate the drop volley or softly angled underspin volley. These volleys can also create more time for you and your teammate to reposition yourselves in an emergency. If, for example, you are pulled very wide on a volley and you hit it back with a great deal of pace, you may not have the time to recover your court position before your opponent strikes the ball. However, if you play the ball softly, or finesse the shot back over the net with underspin, you will give yourself time to prepare for the next ball.

Hitting with finesse is not easy. It requires a soft hand on the racquet—a looser grip—and the technique is made more difficult to master with the titanium and wide-body racquets. These racquets are extremely powerful (and can add many miles per hour to your strokes), but they make learning to take pace off a ball quite a challenge. Nevertheless, it is an art worth mastering because it can create precious time for you and your partner, and because finesse is always the "fake 'em out of their shoes" element of surprise guaranteed to wrong-foot even the most skillful foe.

In general, never be too ambitious for the situation at hand. Many times a moderate and controlled racquet speed will do the job. Experienced players resist the temptation to be a hero on every volley, choosing instead to win the point with an unglamorous but effective placement into the open court. Fence-bashers believe that bone-crushing pace is beautiful. Successful doubles teams know that discretion is always the better part of true heroism on the court. There are no points for style in tennis. Ask yourself a question: Whom would you rather face across the net? Would you rather face a couple of bruisers who think all balls should be crushed and pulverized? Or would you rather face a team who mixes pace with finesse and has you constantly off balance? "Shotmakers" are the most feared species in tennis.

## ANTICIPATION MEANS NO MORE SCRAMBLING

Skilled teams never look rushed, for two reasons: (1) they use the time they make available to themselves, and (2) their racquet-reading skills permit them to move in an indicated direction before the opponent has completed his shot. The lack of last-minute, frantic scrambling to reach a ball is commonly referred to as "anticipation." Players who are said to have great anticipation are not lucky guessers, but rather astute racquet-watchers who have learned to glean enough information from what they see to glide into position before the ball actually arrives. Good anticipation gives a team the luxury of taking all available time to execute a shot and remain unflustered.

On page 8, Jack Kramer was quoted as wishing that his "dream" doubles partner possessed a "feel" for anticipation, and he suggested that the skill has four components:

1. placement of your own shot
2. knowledge of the types of strokes an opponent prefers
3. concentration on the opponent's motions as he is striking the ball
4. the capacity to shift position to meet the return

Consider each of these points carefully:

## Placement of Your Own Shot

By understanding the geometry of the court, you can place shots that let you position your team for the returns your opponent has the *highest* probability of executing. Meanwhile, you should ignore your opponents' return options that have the lowest chance of success.

Court geometry means that angles beget angles. For example, balls hit up the middle will generally come back down the middle. The first step in learning to anticipate an opponent's return is to know and play for what nine out of ten players will hit. For example, when out of position, a player will lob. When presented with options, a player will generally try to drive the ball, usually up the middle, because "pound the middle" has been the doubles mantra for years. When presented with the opportunity to hit a sharply angled volley because a player is standing in his own alley, he will almost always take it.

A word of caution: The concept of *time* is again of crucial importance. If you take away an opponent's timing space, his ball will have to rise if it is to clear the net. If that player is positioned on the baseline, his ball *will* be a lob; his ball *will* be one the terminator can close on and put away. Know this, move before the ball is struck, and you will have *anticipated* the response. If, however, you give an opponent all the time he needs to choose any one of many possible responses, none of the above is viable, and your team is simply helpless, or to use the vernacular, "You guys are dead meat."

## Know Your Opponent's Preferred Strokes

Knowing an opponent's preferred strokes is easy if you meet him in every tournament. The idiosyncrasies, preferences, and habits of a first-time opponent may take you a set to master, but be patient. You will see that almost all players have a pattern of shots they use in sequence or they have a "pet" shot. Once you see a response in a particular tactical situation, play for that shot in every similar situation. Never think "surely he'll do something different this time" until you *see* something different. Players believe in their idiosyncrasies passionately and are reluctant to change them. A player who loves his down-the-line service return will continue to hit it, even if you are standing in the alley, because he believes in his shot more than he believes in your ability to cover it adequately.

## Concentrate on Your Opponent's Motions

You must concentrate with diligence on your opponent and his racquet to pick up the necessary indications of ball placement. If he is about to hit a groundstroke, you must observe not only his racquet preparation but also his foot placement and shoulder turn. If he is about to volley, you need *only* watch the racquet because racquet angle determines where the volley goes, regardless of whether a player is aiming a ball intentionally or simply reacting accidentally.

Jack Kramer states that "these details may appear to be complicated, but after practice they can be noted at a glance." In my experience, I would say that inexperienced students have a great deal of trouble mastering this skill. Most worry that they are unable to fathom some mysterious, transcendental revelation that racquet watching communicates to the rest of the world. But after many court hours, you will be able to see the adjustments in your opponent's physical stance and see the ball come off a racquet at a certain angle. You will find that you have ample time to prepare to hit the ball. It isn't that *watching* the racquet gives you a magical head start, but that *not* watching it will give you no time to prepare your racquet or adjust your court position.

## Shift Position to Meet the Return

Finally, strict attention to your team's crosscourt and terminator court positions (see chapter three) will ensure that all high-percentage strokes aimed at you will never land unplayed on your side of the net. Remember to stay positioned in the *middle* of the probable angles of return using the netstrap and the mirror. Do not cheat your position to defend against the opponent's difficult-to-execute, low-percentage shot. If your team is positioned to intercept what you perceive to be your opponent's most likely responses and to concede the most difficult shots on the court, you will win the match.

Anticipation takes time to develop. There is no time to study probabilities and assess options in the heat of battle; thus trial and error is the only learning method. Determination and a great deal of patience will ultimately pay great dividends.

## TWO RULES OF PROPER COURT MOVEMENT

All great doubles players look as if they are gliding around the court on ice skates. This impression comes from their ability to keep their bodies over their feet and to change directions effortlessly. To look like a great doubles player, you must *always* do the following two things and consider them rules not to be broken.

## Rule 1: Incorporate a Split-Stop

The first rule of proper movement on the court is that you must incorporate a *split-stop* (also called a *split-step*, *check-step*, or, as one of my students said, "a pause for no more than a heartbeat") into your game. A split-stop is when you stop your feet and bring them together every time an opponent strikes a ball. It lets you move in any one of four directions— forward, left, right, or backward—and react to your opponent's ball in a balanced and controlled manner. Failure to make a split-stop is the main reason inexperienced players lunge at balls and find themselves flailing when they should be choosing appropriate responses. For all good players, this momentary pause is absolutely automatic and is never omitted. Unless they are serving, all good doubles players execute the split-stop upon hearing the opponent's racquet strike the ball. However, if you are serving, split-stop when your ball *lands* in the service box. In theory, this is the only time in a doubles point that the ball will *bounce*, and stopping earlier will allow you more time to adjust direction or rate of speed toward the net on a particularly wide or low return of service. With this exception, all good doubles players split-stop on the sound of the ball every single time it is struck by an opponent. This means that if you are the server's partner, there may be a service return and perhaps two or three volleys aimed at your partner. While you have not played a single ball, you will have made three or four split-stops. You can never afford to be moving when your opponent is striking a ball because the odds of being wrong-footed or of running into the ball are simply too great. Split-stopping on impact across the net will allow you to move in any direction with grace and balance.

## Rule 2: Always Move to and Through Each Shot

The other component to the "ice-skating" effect created by good players is that they are always moving forward. To become a great doubles player you must learn not only to move *to* a ball but also *through* it. To emulate these players, learn to return serve while moving forward and to hit your first volley while moving toward the net. (Remember: All approach shots to the net are hit while moving forward, and in doubles, both your service return and your first volley are technically approach shots.) This is not license to run through all of your shots, but to be effective, you must give up the "stop, turn, step, hit" mentality.

To maintain your balance while moving through these shots, to be an ice skater and not a leaning-over lunger who "squats and swats," practice setting your weight on your pivot foot at the very instant you strike the ball. For instance, if you are a right-handed player hitting a backhand service return or first volley, gather your weight on your left leg just as the racquet meets the ball, and then immediately continue forward onto your right leg.

Split-stops, movement forward (in a balanced and controlled fashion at an appropriate rate of speed), agility (not foot speed), and proper use of the pivot foot all combine to give the great doubles player the look of a graceful skater.

## THE GIFT OF GREAT HANDS

One of the things said consistently of the greatest doubles players is that they have "great hands." Unfortunately, this ability is difficult to teach. That is not to say that you can't learn it or cannot be a master of the game of doubles without this gift, but it is a wonderful asset if you have it. Players with great hands seem to have a knack for reflexing balls that would otherwise be putaways back across the net. They display uncommon concentration in situations that would have ordinary mortals bailing out and running for the sidelines. They have either: (1) unique racquet-watching skills and superior knowledge of where the opponent will likely try to put the ball, (2) great luck, (3) tremendous "feel" and instinct for net play, or (4) all of the above. In any event, if you are lucky enough to have a player of this caliber for a partner, make sure you buy him a birthday present. His skill is worth several points a game.

## THE SUM OF THE PARTS

The easy grace, air of confidence, and appearance of great reserves of ability of a great doubles team result not just from many practice hours but from actual time on the court gaining match experience. There are no shortcuts to mastery. If it were possible to take two human beings and teach them every skill needed to execute every shot perfectly on the doubles court, they would be technically perfect yet unable to beat anybody. To achieve mastery, your team must gain, through time, its own character and style—intangibles that are direct results of the number of hours, days, and years you have played the game. *Sprezzatura* develops slowly and cannot be purchased at any price.

The seasoned, experienced, and successful doubles team expresses a wholeness and harmony in its artistic execution of movements that in less-skilled teams look awkward and clumsy.

Efficiency of movement, the confidence to take your time, proper balance and a low center of gravity while moving forward, good anticipation, and the gift of "great hands" are intangibles that will give your doubles team the look of mastery and the visage of winners who will strike fear and terror in the hearts of your opponents.

Mastering the art of doubles takes time, patience, and dogged determination. The skills develop slowly, improving at times by entire levels, and at others by only inches. The struggle is worth it, I think, because it will make your results so much more rewarding. More importantly, I believe the process will teach you to love the game passionately. The best thing to give to an endeavor is your love, and next is your labor. When you can combine them, the product is indeed a very rich experience.

Recently, I had the privilege of meeting Louise Brough, Wimbledon doubles champion and U.S. Open champion with Margaret Osborne duPont from 1942–1950 and from 1955–1958. Her humility and graciousness were charming. When I asked her which of all of her titles meant the most to her, she replied, "All of them, my dear. Every single one."

---

**Intangibles Checklist**

- ☐ Acquire the graceful efficiency of a great doubles team, *sprezzatura*, through strict discipline and mastery of certain "intangibles."
- ☐ Develop your racquet-watching skills to anticipate an opponent's shot and to gain time for your own. Use all available time to hit your shots.
- ☐ Master depth, pace, and finesse to keep from over- or underplaying your own shots and to rob the opposition of the time they need to execute shots properly.
- ☐ Know that developing good anticipation is a necessity and is learned slowly and painfully through experience.
- ☐ Master the split-stop and force yourself to keep pressure on your opponents by relentlessly moving forward.
- ☐ Don't hurry the process of becoming a great doubles team. You cannot play masterful matches before it is time.

---

*The Art of Doubles*

# 10

# Achieving Mental Toughness

..............................

*It is not the critic who counts. … The credit belongs to
the man who is actually in the arena … who at the best,
knows the triumph of high achievement, and who, at the worst,
if he fails, at least he fails while daring greatly, so that his
place shall never be with those cold and timid souls who
knew neither victory nor defeat.*

..............................

*Theodore Roosevelt*

Sports psychology is a developing discipline whose experts have toughened the psyches of tennis players, football teams, baseball pitchers, and basketball stars. Masters in the field have published volumes on the importance of relaxation techniques, proper breathing patterns, rituals, and positive imaging.

This chapter will not amplify their fine work but rather analyze some of the peripheral problems that prevent doubles teams from achieving mental toughness. It also discusses some of the strategies that have helped my students and me overcome performance anxiety.

Imagine you and your partner are embroiled in a tough match against gritty opponents. The match has been a real test of wills, but you have managed to break serve at four all in the third set, and you are now serving for the match. After you have hit several double faults, produced a couple of weak serves, and after your partner has missed several poaches and hit a few shaky volleys, the score is five all. Both you and your partner feel the need for a respirator. What happened?

# THE ANGST AND AGONY OF CHOKING

This phenomenon is commonly referred to as *choking*, or having an "iron elbow," but what does it really mean? When a player chokes a point, he has allowed himself to succumb to what he perceives to be the overwhelming importance of the situation. His breathing becomes irregular, his legs turn to rubber, and his muscles, literally, cease to obey the commands from his brain. Fear becomes the overriding emotional state, and the body does not differentiate between fear for one's very life and fear that one cannot serve a tennis ball over the net on this particular point. It senses danger and reacts by constricting blood vessels and muscles and going to a red alert. It is no wonder that a server choking before a match point can't get the service toss to leave his hand, or if it does, it flies ten feet behind him. In this psychological state, a smooth service toss is impossible. The muscles simply can't obey.

Every player chokes points, and you and your partner should acknowledge this, dismiss those points as part of the natural flow of the match, and get on with the business of winning. Every match contains peaks and valleys. If, however, your team chokes games, sets, or matches, then you are not capable of turning those important and stressful situations into challenges to play your best tennis. You should evaluate the psychological health of your team, identifying patterns of choking or circumstances that create losing syndromes.

That server who frittered away a chance to win the match at 5-4 in the third set with a pitiful display of double faults and shaky volleys was probably secretly saying to himself, "Please, God, let them make four mistakes in a row, and it will be over." What in fact befell this server, and no doubt his partner too, was an anxiety attack that made them stop playing to win, and instead start playing simply not to lose. This primarily occurs when a team is ahead, not behind, in the score. At 4-4, or even 4-5, your team is still embroiled in the battle and focused on your jobs on the court. Your only burden is staying in the match, an onus much easier to bear than the responsibility for winning the set, which you would carry if you were ahead 5-4. When your team is one game away from victory, it is incumbent upon you to actively *win* the match—to continue to take risks under the pressure of needing to close out the match. Great doubles teams are experts at this, but inexperienced teams who have played a brilliant match up to this point will often fail to deliver that masterful, aggressive performance at this crucial juncture where it is most needed.

## CONQUERING THE TWO GREATEST FEARS ON COURT

Fear of losing and fear of winning are different maladies that are born of disparate causes. Sometimes they go together, and sometimes they don't, but they are often present even before the match begins.

Fear of losing is a much more common problem when you play a team you or others feel you should beat. Often, before you ever take the court, devilish thoughts are bouncing off the walls of your psyche:

"Oh, my God, what will people say if we lose to *these* guys?"

"I won't be able to explain it if they even take a set from us."

"If we lose this one, the world will collapse into raucous and hysterical laughter, and I will be absolutely mortified."

Already, before the first ball has been struck in the warm-up, the seeds of self-destruction are in place, and optimum performance may not be possible for you on this day. Once this downward spiral begins, it is very difficult to reverse. Lack of confidence breeds fear of losing, which triggers fear of embarrassing yourselves, which puts two monster egos on the court instead of two tennis players, which makes losing the match a distinct possibility. All of this combines to create that sick feeling in the pit of your stomach that whispers the simple truth: "This ranks right up there with having a root canal, and I *really* don't want to be here."

The following are strategies for overcoming performance anxiety associated with fear of losing.

## Conversations With the Monkey

To hear my students tell the stories of their losses on the occasions that I couldn't be there to watch their matches, you would think that somehow professional players sneaked their way into league competition. Routinely their litanies included:

"*Every* lob they hit grazed the back line."
"Their serves were so good we couldn't even return them."
"Their service returns were bullets. They were just so awesome."

I remained skeptical. This kind of acquiescence is dangerous, and as I saw this attitude being perpetuated by some of my most talented doubles teams, I realized that they were often unable to hold big leads in matches or to convert match points. I decided to try something. To combat these untimely negative thoughts and crises of confidence, I hit upon the idea of the monkey.

If I were to tell a team not to have negative thoughts during an important match, it would be tantamount to saying, just as they were about to take the court, "And oh, by the way, Sandy and Lisa, make sure you don't think about pink elephants." Of course, thousands of pink elephants wearing tutus would frolic endlessly before their eyes for two hours. All good sports psychologists and experts in mental toughness training will say that in order to eliminate negative thinking, one must first acknowledge the existence of these thoughts. Thus, the monkey.

I told all of my teams that each individual player had a monkey on her shoulder and that this arrangement was permanent, so each had better name her monkey and become acquainted. I explained that just as things got tight in a match, or even just as victory was peeking around the corner, this monkey would begin to spout endless drivel such as:

"You cannot possibly keep playing this well."

ALICIA HAS MADE FRIENDS WITH HER MONKEY, AND FEEDING
HIM WELL MAY KEEP THE MATCH UNDER HER CONTROL.

" You're just lucky. They're better than you are."

"You're finished now. They're catching up."

"You can't buy a service return."

"Maybe if they close their eyes and lay down on the court,
   you can win a point."

The possibilities are endless, but they got the idea. I explained that you
cannot ever tell the monkey to shut up because he or she simply will not.
I asked them to acknowledge the presence of the monkey, and his or her
accompanying negativity, and say to the little beast, "Yeah, I know you're
there. I wondered when you would pipe up, but listen, I've got a match to
win here, and I'm going to do it in spite of what you spew at me." Verbal-
izing negative thoughts and feelings helps to dispel them.

Often the monkey's dialogue can be very subtle. Once I asked one of my players, who had just completed probably the finest first set I have ever seen her play, what happened in the second set, because her play had deteriorated so significantly. She said she had no idea. When I asked if she had started to doubt herself, she replied, "No. All I thought was, 'Wow, I sure am playing well after this foot operation.'" This very subtle "monkey speak" is quite enough to send any competitor into a huge downward spiral. I also cautioned the players about those monkeys who are clever enough to become ventriloquists. The gamesmanship employed during the match by opponents of dubious ethics is really very clever "monkey speak:"

"How do you hit that serve so hard?"

"Have you changed your forehand since we last played?"

"How can you drink water with so much ice in it? It would give me a stomachache."

This shrewd "monkey speak" is devilishly designed to get an opponent thinking about anything but winning a match. A stomachache or a forehand gone south is on the horizon.

In the end, I suggested that all of my players get on intimate terms with their personal monkeys. I encouraged them to feed and water the little critters, name them, and with any luck they might sleep through the next match.

The monkey concept is just one way of curtailing negativity on the court that can result in fear of losing. A team can crumble if the players feel that they are fighting more than just the opponents across the net. Fear and low esteem are contagious and must be eliminated if the team is to be successful. Not every strategy works for each team, and players need to be resourceful in devising methods to combat negativity. Several months ago, I e-mailed a team who had gone off to play a national tournament and asked how they fared. The more timid of the two under pressure replied with just one sentence: "George slept through the match."

## Play the Ball, Not the People

The next thing you and your partner should do to avoid this self-destructive spiral is to leave your egos at home and convince yourselves that all opponents are worthy of your complete respect, even if you find they don't even know how to keep score. Never compare your expertise with that across the net. Ignore it and remember that you are playing the *ball*, not the people. The ball may come off your opponents' racquets in a most disconcerting manner, but your challenge is to respond to those oddities, not to blame the people for hitting balls in an unorthodox style.

## Get Centered in the "Now"

Once the match has started, get out of your head and into the match, and stay there. All good sports psychologists agree that in order to give an optimum performance it is vital that you stay centered in the now. There are many excellent training methods for achieving that state. Choose one that enables you to rid yourself of past ("I can't believe how poorly I played that last point") and future ("How can I win my serve next time?") concerns. Concentrate fully on the next point and nothing else.

## Focus on Your Court Job

When the match gets tight, stay positive and confident with your shoulders back and posture erect, and concentrate only on your job on the court. Stay determined to execute your responsibility in each court position without worrying about the consequences of mistakes. If you remain calm and focused and doggedly discharge your duties as you know them, the match will play itself, and the outcome will take care of itself. It takes many hours of match play before a team can finally grasp that if you have the confidence to hit your shots against inferior opponents, you will win, and if you allow fear to keep you from executing properly, you most definitely will lose. It's your choice.

# CONQUER YOUR FEAR OF WINNING

When you find that you are playing "up," with nothing to lose against the team seeded number one, things are much easier, until you wake up and realize you are winning. One of the greatest sources of fun a team can have in a match, with the possible exception of playing "in the zone" and pulverizing your opponents, is playing in a situation where you are not expected to win, and playing well enough to scare the opposition but never being in any danger of winning. This is the classic "no pressure because we've got nothing to lose" scenario in which you and your partner probably play some of your very best tennis.

All is well until this "very best tennis" is suddenly good enough to make the match very close. Then, alas, the fear of winning, the fear of being successful against all odds, rears its ugly head. The symptoms are exactly like those of "fear of losing," but the small, destructive voices are singing different tunes:

"Hey—they were ranked number one last year, and we're up 4-1 in the first set. Oh, my God ..."

"Gee, this isn't so hard. Maybe we're really as good as they are? No way ..."

"What are they waiting for? Surely they have some secret weapon we haven't seen yet ..."

"If we win this ... if we beat them ... if we really win this ... if we win ... oh, but we couldn't possibly beat them ..."

Unlike fear of losing, fear of winning generally sets in after a match has begun. In this case, stellar play begins to deteriorate when the possibility of winning becomes feasible. The downward spiral begins with faltering confidence in the face of unexpected success, leading to tentative shot making, which allows the "favored" team back in the match, permitting you both to believe that winning one set was more than you had hoped for anyway. This attitude, ultimately, ensures the expected loss of the match and explains why the scores of underdog teams against seeded teams are often losses of 7-5, 6-1, or 7-6, 6-0, or even 4-6, 6-1, 6-0. Here are four ways to prevent fear of winning:

1. Build up a generous measure of confidence bordering on cockiness to offset your team's and others' lopsided expectations for the outcome. Fear of success is a very real psychological phenomenon experienced by any doubles team on the court battling not only theoretically superior opponents, but also that team's confidence and reputation.

2. Imagine the match as the opportunity you have worked for and rightfully earned. Do not be content with thinking that at least you have made a good showing and made it a close match. Welcome the chance to prove your worth. Do not shrink from it.

3. Stick with your "job on the court," recognizing that a potential upset situation may elicit an even better performance from a worthy opponent.

4. Embrace the chance to turn your game up a notch to keep pace with determined foes. You may not win this kind of a match the first time you try, but you will sleep well knowing that you battled toe to toe with a favored team, rather than admit that you folded your tent early and mentally tiptoed off the court in defeat before the last point was over.

## Seize the Day

When your team is pitted against a team of equal ability and the outcome of the match is seen as a toss-up, you must not only be mentally tough, but you must also be eagerly searching for ways to seize the momentum of the match.

"Watchers" and "wonderers" tend to ignore the importance of momentum and often attribute close wins to luck and close losses to "that one net-cord 'let' ball that fell your way." On the other hand, one of my league teams, "The Competitors," feels that momentum is such an important dimension they have emblazoned *carpe diem* as a team motto on their sweatshirts. Making things happen in a tight match really depends on your team's ability to seize the day.

In a contest between two even teams, it is unrealistic to expect to grasp the momentum early in the first set and keep it until the conclusion of the match. The tug of war for psychological control continues well into the second or third set, the balance often shifting in favor of one team or another as many as four or five times. In the end, the team that capitalizes on the opportunity to win many points in a row, without making unnecessary errors that negate their advantage, will prevail.

So many times, a team will break serve by waging a monumental battle only to drop their own service game without winning a point. If you are to seize momentum in a match, you must recognize a service break as an opportunity to punish your opponents psychologically. Do everything you can not to relax mentally in a situation that demands added care and concentration.

If you have just won an exhausting service game after being down 0-40, you have some degree of momentum at this stage of the match, particularly because your opponents are probably kicking themselves for having let that game get away. Don't let them regain the control they have just given you. You will be tempted to heave a sigh of relief and relax after the tension of the previous game. It only takes you and your partner missing two service returns and your opponents getting a net-cord winner to arrive at 40-0; the match is now psychologically even again.

## Go for the Jugular

If you are to be truly mentally tough and eager to seize the momentum of a match, anytime you detect a chink in the armor you must go for the jugular. Here are four ways to do just that:

1. When the net man misses a poach off your partner's return, hit your next return right at him—not to cause bodily injury, but because he might be so concerned with his previous error that he will miss again.
2. If you detect that an opponent is feeling shaky about his serve, stand near the service line when you receive to let him know his nervousness is no secret. Nervous servers will often catch two or three service tosses or sigh heavily after a double fault.
3. Whenever you are the lucky recipient of a net-cord let winner, try hard not to even the score by losing the next point carelessly.

4.  If you see that an opponent lacks confidence, play most of your shots in his direction whenever possible.

These tactics are not immoral or unethical in any way. They are strategies for exercising psychological superiority over your opponents, and thus over the match. If it is true that 65 percent of tennis is mental, as has often been said, then your ability to dominate psychologically and ultimately seize and retain the momentum of a match is much more important than your stroke production.

## THE ZONE

Whenever I watch a Super Bowl, I remember what is referred to in the Bay Area as "The Drive." I don't remember exactly what year it was, but with hardly any time left on the clock, Joe Montana led the 49ers down the field against the Cincinnati Bengals for a winning touchdown drive. The extraordinary thing about that moment was that everyone—coaches and players on both sides of the field and the spectators—knew that Montana was going to get that score. Why? Because he had the uncanny ability to put himself into the zone whenever he needed to. He could transport himself into that marvelous state at will. The really good news is that the zone is a real place, and you, too, can learn to cross that threshold when you are most in need.

If you talk to anyone who has been there, or if you have experienced it yourself, you will find that there are three characteristics in common to all who have entered that special state of mind:

• The ball is as big as a grapefruit.
• Time has slowed down.
• There is a feeling of invincibility.

Underlying this mystical state is a sense of supreme confidence coupled with complete relaxation. For most of us, this happens rarely and unbidden. And when it does, you know it and you wish you could bottle it because you know that victory is certain.

Rather than awaiting another surprise visit someday, the really, really good news is that you *can* bottle it. Think about the last time, or the only time, you were in the zone. Try to recall what your facial expression conveyed. If you don't know, ask your partner. Most people recall a smile on their face, but it could have been anything to a frown to a face devoid of expression. It is important to find that expression and file it. Next, assign it a word. Any word will do, but it must be your own and be able to trigger that facial expression. Lastly, as you speak the word to yourself on the court and arrange your facial expression, caress your racquet with your playing hand. This takes some practice, but it really does work. Many times in my playing career I found myself having to perform under the pressure generated by hundreds of spectators. When I came off the court, I would always seek out a friend and ask if anyone clapped. If they had, I had not heard them at all.

If you have never been in the zone, be patient. You *will* be visited by this incredible phenomenon. It rarely occurs in a fun match, preferring to appear when you are under pressure. If one day you suddenly realize that things are easy, the ball is huge, time has slowed down, and you have no doubt that you will win, stop and assess things. How do you feel? Are you smiling? What word best describes your euphoria? Bottle it. You now have the tools to summon the zone at will. Fear of winning will be a distant memory.

## REMEMBER THESE FINAL WISDOMS

To be mentally tough, your team must display increasing grace and courage as a situation becomes more difficult. No matter how dire the outlook, keep your perspective and be gentle with yourself and your partner. If you are struggling against tough opponents and are fighting yourself or your partner, your team is severely outnumbered. You have enough problems across the net without creating unnecessary obstacles on your own side.

Constant self-criticism or criticism of your partner, although it may be unspoken, indicates that you are measuring your performance against some mythical standard of play that you have set. Learn to play with the weapons you have brought to the court; don't pine for those you left at home. Freeing yourself that day from self-concept removes limitations, so if you didn't manage to bring a blockbuster first serve to the court, it is far more constructive to embrace the capabilities of your second serve than to spend the match berating yourself for not owning something that simply does not belong to you that day. It doesn't mean you *can't* serve. It means that, for whatever reason, you must serve *differently* in that match. If you can't hit a forehand drive on a given day, stop trying. Chip the ball instead. Search your quiver for a different arrow to sling rather than railing against fate for crippling your arsenal.

## Practice Being Tough

Being a mentally tough competitor takes constant practice. It is not a skill like riding a bicycle—learned once and then possessed forever. The expression "match tough" is an important one. It refers to the number of times you have competed under pressure and experienced "closing a match out," coming from behind to win, winning the close one, or winning when it is not expected of you. While you can practice your volleys by drilling in a relaxed atmosphere, mental toughness is the one part of your game that can only be practiced under pressure. In addition, if you don't play pressure-filled matches, your toughness will evaporate. To give a truly tough performance, you not only must have the courage to hit your best shots under pressure, but you must also have practiced those shots enough to ensure a reasonable chance that they will stay in the court when you most need them to—during the big points. When your vanquished opponents call you "match tough," you have arrived.

The year Arthur Ashe won Wimbledon, a reporter found him out on a practice court an hour before the finals of the tournament practicing his serve.

It was an unusually warm day in England, and the reporter watched as Ashe served perhaps one hundred balls, all of which hit some part of a service line. Having served what appeared to be one hundred aces, Ashe picked up all of the balls and proceeded to repeat the entire process. The reporter could stand it no longer and asked him why, if he had just hit every line in the service court, would he want to practice serving another hundred balls in the heat just before a Wimbledon final. Ashe replied, "So that I can hit *one* under pressure."

## Display A Winning Attitude

Mentally tough teams display a winning attitude from the very first point, and it does not go unnoticed by the opposition. Mentally fragile teams convey a willingness to lose without a fight, and it shows. If you think back to the last few matches you played, you can probably point to teams you have encountered who displayed characteristics typical of tough competitors, as well as some that you just knew had no will to win.

Remember, to acquire the character of a team that is psychologically tenacious and unwilling to beat themselves, you must learn that an ugly "W" is *always* better than a pretty "L." Stand out there as long as it takes, and do whatever it takes to win. You don't earn national rankings with pretty strokes.

Winning is definitely more fun than losing, but failure is a necessary part of the learning experience. If you try to learn just one thing every time you lose a match, you can turn those losses into stepping-stones that lead to a more solid performance in the future, and yet, there will always be unexplainable "bad losses." It is an irony of the game that absolute mental toughness and a demeanor impenetrable to the emotional strain of match play is always a goal just out of reach. Achieving mental toughness is a process that is never finished. It is a constantly elusive dream that you grasp by the fingers. Sometimes you hold on. Sometimes you don't. Meanwhile, insecurity and lack of confidence will always nip at your heels.

## Play to Win

Mentally tough teams always play to win. They never play to avoid losing. Above all, they have learned to keep their perspective. They have learned that there are great days, so-so days, and days when racquet-smashing seems like a better sport.

The next time your team is embroiled in a tense match where points have been choked away and the fear of losing or the fear of winning is starting its ugly chant, stop. Stop everything and discuss with your partner how the loss of this one match will seriously, irrevocably, and forever diminish your lives as tennis players, as citizens, as bird-watchers, as PTA members, or as human beings. The answer should make you both relax—and smile.

---

**Mental Toughness Checklist**

- [ ] Everybody chokes points, but if you choke games or matches, take stock of your team's psychological health.
- [ ] Never succumb to the "trying not to lose" syndrome. No matter what the score, force things to happen.
- [ ] Remember that fear of losing can seriously compromise your ability to perform even the easiest tasks under pressure.
- [ ] Learn to embrace your monkey.
- [ ] Remember that fear of winning will cost you the upset win you almost had, but let get away.
- [ ] To become mentally tough, stop the destructive voices in your head and stick to your jobs on the court.
- [ ] Wrest the momentum from tough opponents and seize the day.
- [ ] Learn to call upon the zone at will.
- [ ] The impenetrable armor of absolute confidence at all times is a myth. Mental toughness is a constant struggle needing eternal practice and patience.

---

# 11

# Let's Talk About
# Winning and Losing

..............................

*If you can meet with Triumph and Disaster, and treat
those two imposters just the same. . . .*

..............................

**Rudyard Kipling**
*Engraved over the entrance to center court at Wimbledon*

Well, this is what it's all about, isn't it? You strive to get the court position right, the shot selection perfect, the mental toughness polished to a keen edge, all in the name of leaving the court victorious. And yet, more often than you would like, you lose. Bad hair day? Too much wind? Unbelievably lucky opponents? Or was your performance fatally flawed? Doubles teams very often come off the court not really knowing how that match got away from them. I have observed that humility is endless, and even at nationals, the difference between winning and losing really comes down to the little things. I once read an article in the USPTA (United States Professional Tennis Association) magazine that included an amazing statistic: If you win 50 percent of the points in a set, your chances of winning the set are 50 percent. If you win 55 percent of the points in a set, your chances of winning the set are *95 percent*. Over the years, I have observed mistakes made in common by teams I have coached that came up just a bit short when it mattered the most.

# THE TEN MOST COMMON REASONS
# DOUBLES TEAMS LOSE MATCHES

**1. Never Close the Net and Hit Crosscourt.** In chapter three I explained the perils of the crosscourt player closing the net on a short ball and returning the shot back to the crosscourt opponent. It's one thing to know this on the practice court and an entirely different proposition to think clearly under pressure, knowing instinctively where the ball should go (hit it straight!), and resisting the temptation to play the ball right back to the manipulative crosscourt opponent. The higher the level of competition, whether it be districts, sectionals, nationals, or age-level tournaments, the more you can be sure they are doing this absolutely on purpose. They *love* to sucker you into over-closing the net so that they can lob you. And if you forget the rule that all very short balls must be hit in a straight line when you are the crosscourt player, or your ego falls out of your pocket, you will pay every time, struggling to ignore the giggles across the net.

**2. The Wrong Grip.** Many players don't want to hear this, but a brief discussion of the proper volley grip is really necessary. The *only* grip that can handle low volleys effectively is the continental grip. With rare exceptions, you simply cannot handle a low volley with the all too popular extreme western grips that have become the fashion. The hand is turned completely under the racquet so that the knuckles are facing the court in all western grips. This closes the racquet face and makes a low volley extremely difficult. There are ways to learn to open the racquet face and still hold that western grip, but the truth is that the face remains closed at the moment of impact if, under pressure, you don't remember to make the adjustment consciously and with forethought. And on some crucial point in a tiebreak, when you are distracted by moving into position, it will, it will, it will let you down. It is really worth trying to learn the continental grip for volleys, but make sure to do it slowly. The continental grip is the "carry your briefcase" grip and it allows the racquet face to remain slightly open. It makes handling low volleys very easy. Changing to this grip is a major cause of tennis elbow in players who have never previously experimented with it.

**3. The World of Volleys is Not Divided Equally.** The really bad news for a number of players is that the world is divided into three-quarters backhand volleys and one-quarter forehand volleys. Your forehand volley stops at your right hip (left, of course, if you are a lefty), and *everything* else is a backhand. Crosscourt players moving toward the net will try in vain to make a ball a forehand volley, and they either end up in their partner's lap or on the bench. Terminators deliberately run past poaches to ensure a forehand, but, of course, they miss the shot. The problem is exacerbated if you have a two-handed volley. Any ball aimed right at your navel is a backhand, and this requires the two-handers to take a hand off the racquet or risk shoving the butt cap of the racquet up their noses—an excellent reason to consider learning a one-handed backhand volley. Technically, a backhand volley is an easier shot because your arm is traveling away from you. It also, for the same reason, creates a better angle. Learn to embrace your backhand volley.

**4. To Bounce or Not to Bounce a Ball.** All servers should execute a split-stop at the moment their serve hits the court in their opponent's service box. At this juncture comes that mind-numbing moment: "Should I let this bounce?" The question is actually irrelevant, and players' inability to understand that fact is absolutely the biggest cause of missed first volleys and consequently, lost service games. The actual stroke production for half volleys and low volleys was discussed in chapter four. But the unnecessary time a server takes to decide how to come skidding to the net on his nose to prevent a bounce or backpedal to ensure a bounce, and thus avoid a low volley, is certain to result in a service break at a crucial point in the match. There is no question that players do get somewhat tentative in big games that could decide a set. But the low and half volleys are necessary parts of your arsenal and need to be embraced as routine, although somewhat difficult, tasks to make certain you hold serve at a critical juncture in the set.

**5. Second-Ball Lobitis.** Certain players are prone to getting the "yips" when things get tight in a match, and when that happens, "second ball lobitis" is the unfortunate result. The "yips" is shoptalk for an absolute loss of confidence in all strokes because of the tension of the moment. And when that happens, executing a low volley or a ripping, low crosscourt service return suddenly seems like a task of Herculean difficulty. So what does this poor crosscourt player do? He serves, freezes in his tracks, and lobs the second ball. The simplest crosscourt return suddenly seems like the riskiest of all shots, so he pushes the service return into play, becomes glued to the court, and lobs the second ball. Not once. Not twice. He lobs the second ball for the rest of the set or the match because he believes, in his convoluted state of mind, that this is the safest shot to execute. Actually, it is the most cowardly. The players across the net know it and pound overheads until the match is mercifully over. There is no quick fix for this syndrome, but all coaches are fond of saying that adversity doesn't build character; it reveals it. It would behoove all "second ball lobitis" victims to think very carefully about the risks of taking no risks. The end result is very ugly.

**6. An Inability to Hit a Spin Serve.** Too many players underestimate the importance of learning to put spin on a serve. You need to serve up the middle to allow your partner an opportunity to poach (see chapter five). The higher the level of competition, the more difficult it is simply to put a flat serve up the middle and expect it to elicit a ball your partner can move to and put away. All the best receivers love to get their hands extended on a service return without moving their feet. Flat serves to the middle are often in their "roundhouses"—the perfect place in their strike zones. I have watched many of my players hit flat serves up the middle of the court only to watch helplessly as their partners duck while winning service returns scream past both outstretched racquets. Of course, you could begin to serve wide and hope for a better result, but the better correction is to put spin on your serve. If you add topspin, the receiver will have to start his swing at shoulder height—not in his strike zone. If you add slice, the receiver (right-handed) will either be jammed in the deuce court or stretched out behind his partner in the ad court. All spin serves take the receiver out of his comfort zone and make winning the service game a more manageable task.

**7. Not Trusting the Dimensions of the Court.** The size of the court is a very important concept. Many players believe that the dimensions of their opponents' court are thirty-six feet wide by thirty-nine feet long in practice and six inches wide by eight inches long in a match. They spend many practice hours hitting angled volleys and overheads into alleys, lovely dropshots into small areas of the court just beyond the net, and they work on down-the-line service returns that just clip the outside line. But the minute the main event begins—the minute points count—they play all of their shots right back to the racquets of their opponents because they do not believe any of the afore-practiced shots will stay in the court. It is a long day at the office for these players because they believe that their opponents' court has shrunk to the size of a mere postage stamp while theirs has grown to the size of a football field. What works in practice works in a match, and if you don't use your shots, you will lose them—and the match.

**8. Loss of Momentum.** Momentum is very fragile, and once lost, it is difficult to regain. Loss of momentum is a major culprit when teams lose a big lead in a set, and eventually, the match. If you are alert, there are several things you can do to make sure you keep momentum on your side. If your partner misses a service return, you cannot. Kick it over the net if you must. Missing two or three service returns in a row is like sand draining out of the hourglass. If your team receives a double fault to, say the deuce court, the ad court player *cannot* dump the next return into the net. If you are the lucky recipient of a net-cord winner, don't shank the next ball on the next point. If you prevail in a very, very long point worthy of many high fives, don't double fault on the next point. Match management is critical to keeping momentum on your side of the court.

**9. Preconceived Notions About Opponents.** Heeding other people's well-intentioned but useless chatter about the strengths and weaknesses of your next opponents is a big mistake. One doubles pair I coached was told by well-wishers that the team they were about to face was notorious for their perfect lobs and that they beat everyone by lobbing incessantly. My team was so unnerved that they stayed off the net and didn't even serve and volley, only to discover that they saw no lobs from these people in two entire sets. Another significant danger is to be told that a team you are about to play makes bad line calls. You certainly are going to be more focused on the lines than the ball and be very distracted. Every match sets up differently, and your particular strengths may force opponents renowned for lobs or dinks to alter their strategy entirely. Preconceived notions of opponents' preferences interfere with your ability to do your job on the court. Let things unfold naturally.

**10. Changing a Winning Game Strategy.** Never change a winning strategy. Watch out for this one because it happens all the time and in very subtle ways. Recently, one of my doubles teams was involved in a very close and tough match. They eked out the first set by their clever use of the Australian serving formation. They didn't do it once in the second set or the tiebreak and lost both. If you find something that works and earns points, don't drift away from it. Never get into that awful mind game of, "Well, surely they have this figured out now, so maybe we better try something else." Maybe they have no idea how to combat what you are doing now. Maybe they never will. In competition, always keep two disparate thoughts equally present in your heads: "They are very good, and we are lucky to get a point." And: "They are absolutely stupid until proven otherwise." If you are winning each point when you return serve with a dropshot, why, oh why, would you stop doing it? If it ain't broke. ...

The previous list should be considered a checklist of corrections for the health of your doubles game, or strategic pitfalls to avoid in the heat of battle. Any one of them has been the cause of many an aspiring team's downfall in a crucial situation. Losing can become a habit if you don't learn something from each loss. Above all, when you lose, don't lose the lesson. Peaks and valleys in your career are inevitable. The goal is to achieve a steadier performance.

Winning consistently is a whole lot more fun, but it requires discipline and meticulous preparation. As a coach, I believe that competing well, even when not playing well, is a direct result of faultless preparation.

One year not too long ago, one of my league teams was due to play districts in an unfamiliar city. The day before the tournament started, I insisted that the entire team drive the fifty or so miles to the hosting club. We made court reservations and held our final practice at the site. We got very lost trying to find the club, and when we arrived, we discovered that the court surface was much like playing on a carpet—something my team had no experience with. We were the only team on the courts that day, but the players got oriented to the location and conditions in a way that other teams did not. They went on to sectionals.

Here in Connecticut, league matches are timed, and I devote a fair amount of practice time to clock management, even including ways to thwart stalling opponents and regain the pace of the match. This practice led one of my pairs to pull off an astonishing accomplishment at sectionals not too long ago. It was a day of debilitating heat and horrible humidity, and the tournament was played outside. One of my doubles teams won the first set 7-5, but one of the partners was truly having a heat stroke. After taking all the allowed time-outs, they hit upon the idea of losing the second set 6-0, on purpose, as quickly as they could. Their idea was that rather than retiring, they could manage to get through a ten-point tiebreak much more quickly than a grueling second set. They did it, and they won the match. I could not have been more proud of their initiative. It spoke to the number of hours they had spent preparing for any eventuality. The hours you spend on the practice court will pay huge dividends at times that will surprise you the most.

## THE THREE KEYS TO WINNING

Lofty demands put too much pressure on you, but lofty goals do not. The three keys to optimum performance can be summed up as CPR.

**Confidence.** Confident players enjoy the pressure of a situation, and they are undaunted by the necessity of performing before a crowd, their teammates, or multitudes of fans rooting against them. They maintain their composure in the face of adversity because they know that one bad shot does not make a bad game, that a bad game does not make a bad set, a bad set is not the same thing as a bad match, and a bad match does not make a bad player—just a bad day. They have learned to check their egos at the door and to play with both humility and aggressiveness. They are able to take each point as it comes and are less likely to make subjective judgments about the natural ebb and flow of a match. Confident players are also more able to put themselves in that wonderful place we call the zone (discussed in chapter ten) because they remain upbeat in body language and attitude. Finally, a little swagger doesn't hurt, and with a little behavior modification, even the most fearful competitor can learn to believe.

**Perspective.** No two partners ever come to the court every time they play equipped with every weapon they own. Some days you have a forehand; some days you don't. Some days you are magnificent and your partner stinks. Other days it's the reverse. If the players across the net are painting every line on the court, as hard as you try, it may not be your day. Players who have a good perspective both on their own game and on the current situation are able to evaluate exactly what is going on in the match objectively and dispassionately. They may surmise that the guys across the net are unbelievably lucky, but they don't rail against the fates, the curse of the tennis god, or the sorry state of tennis in the United States. They know they will live to fight another day, and they know that revenge is definitely an option. Wild emotional swings on the court generally serve to exacerbate an already unpleasant experience.

**Resignation.** Great players make great shots at great moments. Why? Because they have accepted the fact that losing is a distinct possibility, and they have already made peace with that potential outcome. It really comes down to one thing, and only one thing: If you perform better than your opponents do, you will win. If you do not, you won't. So it's better to clear the head of the mind chatter and let the body do what it has practiced so hard. Neither be afraid to lose nor afraid to win. Play each match as if it is your last. One day, you're bound to be right, so leave nothing for another day, ever.

When you and your partner know that you have given an optimum performance, and better yet, it has earned you a splendid victory, you have created a moment in your tennis career that you will never forget. As you accumulate these high points, you are making a scrapbook that will be with you for the rest of your life. I will never forget the moment when my service return for a winner meant that our team was going to league nationals. Nor will I ever forget the amazing performances under pressure that sent a league team I coach to their nationals.

Winning is always made much more poignant by the string of losses you have to endure to climb that pinnacle. A number of years ago I attended a seminar by Dan Millman, author of a wonderful book called *The Warrior Athlete*. His presentation was called "The Ten Points for Being Human." Several of them are relevant to the growth and development of a mature and successful doubles team:

1. You will learn lessons—forever.
2. There are no mistakes—only lessons.
3. A lesson is repeated until learned—and they get harder.
4. There are always lessons to be learned.
5. You will tend to forget all of this.

These statements underscore the fact that the journey toward mastery is never finished. It is not that the goal is elusive, but rather that learning to win is a process that is constantly evolving and that the mistakes made along the way are inevitable. The desire to win and compete successfully under pressure can overshadow the value of the lessons to be learned as you near your goal. Peyton Manning, the gifted quarterback of the Indianapolis Colts, has said that pressure is a privilege. It is. Embrace it.

**Winning and Losing Checklist**

☐ Avoid the ten most common reasons teams lose matches:
- Never close the net and hit crosscourt
- The wrong grip
- The world of volleys is not divided equally
- To bounce or not to bounce a ball
- Second-ball lobitis
- An inability to hit a spin serve
- Not trusting the dimensions of the court
- Loss of momentum
- Preconceived notions about opponents
- Changing a winning game strategy

☐ Embrace the three keys to winning: confidence, perspective, and resignation.

# 12

## Choosing the Better Arena to Showcase Your Team's Skills

..................................

*When you come to a fork in the road, take it.*

..................................

*Yogi Berra*

It is a rare team indeed that is content to limit their court time to "hit and giggle" tennis, having rollicking fun and not caring about the outcome of the match. Most doubles teams naturally crave to see how they measure up against others in organized competition. There are two arenas to choose from: league tennis or tournament tennis. Many teams opt to participate in both, but many differences exist between the two formats.

## LEAGUE TENNIS

Like it or not, there is no doubt that adult competitive tennis has become a team sport. The argument for league tennis over tournament tennis is that those players who would pay an entry fee to participate, only to lose in the first round and rarely be guaranteed a consolation round, receive an entire season of league play for the same money. League tennis is *not* single elimination until the team reaches districts. The following experience is fairly typical. Our prototypical player, Beeper Marie Honeyshoes, is a blond, forty-something avid tennis player and a real "wannabe." She has spent thousands of dollars for tournament entry fees and has never won a round. The dream of attaining a national ranking is fading farther and farther into the sunset with each passing year. But Beeper joins a league team. She doesn't win many matches for the team, but the team makes districts anyway. Suddenly the possibility of national champion is within her grasp.

League tennis dangles this carrot in front of anyone's nose, regardless of the level of play or the degree of competence, in a way tournament tennis cannot. League tennis provides players like Beeper Marie with an opportunity to succeed with a losing record. She can say proudly, "No, I didn't win, but the team did."

League tennis is particularly attractive to new doubles teams who have had either very little competitive exposure or very few years on the court. For those who missed the high school or college athletic team experience, being a member of a league team is a heady experience. They may have cheered, but they have never *been* cheered.

One of the biggest advantages of league over tournament tennis is that players compete *only* against their peers, regardless of age. The NTRP (National Tennis Rating Program) computer assigns each player a rating—2.0 being a beginner's rating and 5.0 being close to a professional player—and no player may compete below his assigned rating. If Beeper Marie is designated a 3.5 and the partner she wishes to compete with is rated 4.0, she will have to get another partner, one also rated 3.5 *or lower* because no one is allowed to compete "out of level." The idea behind NTRP ratings is that every match should be a competitive one. Although it can happen, the theory is that no team should ever be blown off the court. Parity is the goal. The measuring stick of your team's improvement is the ability of the computer to increase your rating to the next level based on your annual results. The downside is that you may be bumped up, but your partner may not. You would then have to find a new partner *and* a new team.

There is much camaraderie and social interaction in league tennis. Usually, the team chooses a name and a team uniform. Often there are pre- and post-season parties for the players and their spouses or significant others. Each home team provides food and, often, wine and beer, to be enjoyed after the match by the home and visiting teams. Weekly team practices provide an opportunity for all team members to get acquainted and share war stories. A sense of belonging engenders team pride and loyalty. For those doubles teams that seek to be part of a group of twenty or twenty-five like-minded competitors, league is a wonderful thing.

But, as with any enterprise, league has its drawbacks. You may find that you and your partner are not included in match lineups as often as you would prefer. You could also find yourself in a lineup but not scheduled to play with your regular partner. With a team of twenty-plus players, some of whom will be singles specialists (except in senior league, which begins at age 50), everyone is clamoring for playing time. The coach or captain must weigh the desire to win matches against the necessity to give all team members a spot in the lineup.

League is a very local endeavor until the team earns the right to go to sectionals. This is not necessarily a drawback, but in a twelve-match season, your team will probably play the same opposing teams twice. The members of the other teams in your flight (consisting of about six teams) are likely to be very familiar adversaries. Even districts, the first rung on the ladder to nationals, is a largely local affair. It is unlikely that you and your partner will face unfamiliar opponents until your team gets to sectionals.

League tennis spans a long period of time. It begins in May and finishes in July. Districts and sectionals begin in August, and should you be so lucky, nationals are held in October. There are essentially four steps to complete before you can claim the title of national champion. Your team must do well enough from May to July to qualify for districts, which is the first of a three-part-single-elimination tournament. One team emerges as the district winner to move on to sectionals, and that winner earns the right to represent an

IT DOESN'T HAVE TO BE THE ROAD *LESS TRAVELED,* IT JUST HAS
TO BE THE *BETTER* ROAD FOR YOU AND YOUR PARTNER. TRYING
BOTH MAY BE THE BEST SOLUTION.

entire section of the country at nationals. Should your team come through
the tournament as that fortunate representative, it faces one more huge
obstacle. For most teams, nationals are a very long plane trip away. In 2006,
they were in Hawaii. Team members are loath to make that kind of a trip if
they aren't going to play. The coach or captain should be very clear about
lineups, subs, and spectators before plane reservations are made. There is
no question that difficult decisions must be made, and feelings will be hurt.
The year that my 3.0 team made nationals, I told them that anyone who
boarded the plane to Arizona would play. It was the right decision because,
although I knew they had the talent to win it all, I correctly surmised that
they would be just so thrilled to have made it and so enthralled with the
cacti that their performance would be less than stellar.

Whether your preference is men's, women's, mixed, or senior doubles,
or the entire package, league offers the team-oriented doubles pair a
great experience.

## TOURNAMENT TENNIS

League tennis offers doubles teams a subjective measurement of their ability to perform against similarly assessed players. Tournament tennis offers an immediate and objective evaluation of a team's ability: You win, you move on. You lose, you're out. However, increasingly over the past fifteen years, doubles teams that wish to pursue the individual goal of a sectional or national ranking have found that tournaments in their respective age groups are few, small, or canceled at the last minute due to lack of entries. Even "open" tournaments, those that might include college players, have dwindled due to the growing popularity of league tennis. Tournament participation is a much more solitary endeavor, sometimes requiring hours of travel time. Often, it is just you and your partner sitting together at an unfamiliar club, miles from home. But usually the clubs that make the effort to hold a tournament are the nicest facilities in the area, and they go to a great deal of trouble to be hospitable.

One of the advantages of playing tournaments is that you play when *you* want to play, not when a captain needs you for a league lineup. Many tournaments still adhere to the full three-set format—something all players miss since league tennis replaced it with a third-set, ten-point tiebreak. Some even include a consolation or feed-in draw so that you are guaranteed at least a second match against other losers if you are eliminated from the main event. Even if you draw the number-one seed in the first round, at least you have paid for the opportunity to face excellent opponents you would otherwise never play. If it is unlikely that this team would even consider calling you for a practice match, then look at it as a chance to display your skills at the big-league level. You have nothing to lose. Tournaments also provide instant gratification. If you win, you get to hoist the trophy on the last day of play instead of waiting months for that honor. Tournaments are also more exciting because each round is an elimination round, and your tennis ego is at stake every time you take the court. Needing to win to continue playing is a much more immediate experience than that afforded by the ongoing league season.

Tournament tennis comes in many varieties, but the two most common are: open and senior competition. The Open tournaments are usually filled with college-level players vying for rankings and are very tough sledding for those who are over twenty years old and who have not previously played college tennis. The "senior" designation begins at age twenty-five and continues through the eighty-and-over bracket. Many players prefer playing senior tennis to all other venues. While the ability levels may vary widely, the players across the net from you are your peers in age, interests, and background. This engenders a feeling of camaraderie and encourages respect for opponents. Many doubles teams create lifelong friendships playing this circuit.

If you and your partner decide to try tournaments, play at least one national event on a surface unfamiliar to you. There is no prequalification requirement to play a national tournament. All you have to do is pay your entry fee and show up. If you play hard-court tennis, play a national grass-court event. It is an experience you will never forget, and it will give you an appreciation of the difficulty of adjusting your game to an untrue bounce. It is a good idea to learn to play on all surfaces, each of which requires very different shot selection.

Many teams find that a combination of league and tournament tennis suits their competitive careers perfectly. That way, they get to see their tournament rankings published at the end of the year in the Tennis Yearbook, and they still experience the league team's success. In the end, it's all about the quest for the Holy Grail—a trip to nationals for the league team and a victory in the finals for a tournament competitor. Be sure to enjoy the journey.

## League or Tournament Checklist

☐ League tennis offers a team-oriented experience.
☐ Tournament tennis is a more solitary endeavor.
☐ League matches are usually played locally.
☐ Tournaments can take you all over the country.

# 13

# Drills for Honing Your Skills

..................................

*Practice is the best of all instructors.*

..................................

*Publilius Syrus*

By practicing only a little bit, or without enthusiasm, you can gradually let the task of improving your skills overwhelm you. It is a misconception to believe that you can actually practice technical skills while playing points. Conversely, the mental skills—communication and mental toughness—can only be honed and improved under the pressures of match play.

This chapter contains some suggestions for drills to improve the skills enumerated in this book. I have used all of them successfully in my teaching. The drills are grouped together under the chapter headings for which they are most appropriate. Most of the drills are interchangeable, however, and can be used to sharpen more than just one skill. However you choose to practice, keep it relevant. Never practice what you aren't going to use in a match.

## EMOTIONAL, TECHNICAL, AND BALANCE (CHAPTER ONE), COMMUNICATION (CHAPTER TWO), AND MENTAL TOUGHNESS (CHAPTER TEN)

The only way to practice the mental side of tennis—the teamwork, the communication skills, and the toughness under pressure—is to make the commitment to play in practice exactly the way you want to play in a very important match. It is difficult to resist the temptation to play "hit and giggle" tennis when you are playing just for fun, but the art of winning takes practice.

When playing practice matches, try to create some tension in the situation. Arrange to play people who are better than you whenever possible. Play for lunch or a drink, and sign up for court number one, where people congregate to watch the action, instead of court number eighteen out near the parking lot. Practice situational responses. If it is break point and you are receiving serve, hit the very same shot you want to hit in the finals of the nationals. If you are serving at 30-40, hit the serve you need to capture a number-one ranking. Take the same amount of time between points as you would if the match really mattered, and communicate with one another about a plan of attack as if your whole season hinged on winning this match. The ability to perform intelligently and calmly under pressure will not be there when you need it if you have to invent it on the spur of the moment. Like your forehand, it must be practiced. Play seriously in practice, play "up" when you can, and try never to lose.

## Shadow Doubles Drill

To help you gain this confidence under pressure, use a crosscourt drill with your partner in which you, as server, get only one serve, which *must* go in, and in which you *cannot* miss your first volley. Your partner, the receiver, *must* get the service return in play and *must* make his first volley, after which the point is over. This drill is called shadow doubles because neither player has a partner. Under pressure, most points are lost on the third ball, and if each of you can be confident that you can always properly execute two balls, you will begin to play those important points with great assurance. Remember, there is no job for the terminator if the crosscourt player does not start the point correctly.

## The Everything-Is-Good Drill

This drill will help you to develop better concentration and avoid making costly mental mistakes. Four players actually play points and keep score, but *every* ball on the court is deemed "good," whether it in fact bounces out or not. Play only stops when a ball hits the net or bounces twice. Players will find themselves playing long serves and chasing lobs that are really out, but it is a great drill for increasing hustle, avoiding the "oh, I thought it was going to be out" error, and for overall levels of concentration throughout an entire point.

## PROPER COURT POSITION (CHAPTER THREE) AND NET CONTROL (CHAPTER SIX)

### Take-Away-the-Net Drill

This is the best drill for court position, along with its more sophisticated variations. One team begins in its proper crosscourt and terminator volley positions, while the team across the net is positioned defensively—that is, behind the baseline. The net team must maintain their netstrap and mirroring obligations while being peppered with drives from the baseline team which is intent upon drilling balls either between the two at the net or passing them in their alleys. The deuce and ad court net players alternate starting as the crosscourt player, and the feed always goes to the player who is in a crosscourt position. If any ball falls unplayed between the net players, or if either the crosscourt player or the terminator is passed in his alley, the team relinquishes the net to the opposition and must retreat to the baseline. Meanwhile, the baseline team practices good defense and looks for errors in direction by the net team that would produce an opportunity to execute the crosscourt lob. No serving is allowed. Each rally is begun with a drop feed, and only one ball per rally is used. Remember the concept of "timing space" (chapter six), and if your court looks like Swiss cheese and you keep losing the net, a gut check on the quality of your volleys is in order.

When you have mastered this drill and it becomes boring, allow the baseline team to try to drive the volleying team off the net by lobbing as well as by hitting passing shots. Now begin to hit ugly volleys as the crosscourt player and drop volleys as the terminator. In this variation, the net team not only must defend against the passing shots but also cannot allow a ball to *bounce behind them*, providing good overhead practice for the crosscourt player and a chance to polish those flash cards—"stay," "switch," or "back" (chapter two). If, however, a lob gets over their heads and bounces, they relinquish the net to their opponents. This drill works both sides of the net quite realistically because a baseline team that has successfully put a ball over the heads of a net team would immediately reclaim the net in actual match play.

## The Identity Drill

This is the most sophisticated version of the take-away-the-net drill. It is so named because it challenges the net team to know who is the crosscourt player and who is the terminator, and why, at all times. The net team begins with both players standing on the service line. Of course, the team would never be even on the court in this position in a real point, but this starting position is an excellent way to determine if both players really know whether to assume the position of the crosscourt player or the position of the terminator. The baseline team begins the drill with a drop feed, alternating feeds to the deuce and ad court players. If the player receiving the feed hits the ball in a straight line, he becomes the terminator, and his partner remains on the service line as the crosscourt player. If, however, he hits the ball crosscourt, he remains on the line while his partner moves into the terminator position (see diagrams thirty-four and thirty-five). Under fire, players do make directional errors and should be

**Diagram 34**
## The Identity Drill:
## Scenario One

In this identity drill, the deuce court player has chosen to hit her volley in a straight line. This makes her the terminator, so she follows her ball to the net and her partner holds the crosscourt position.

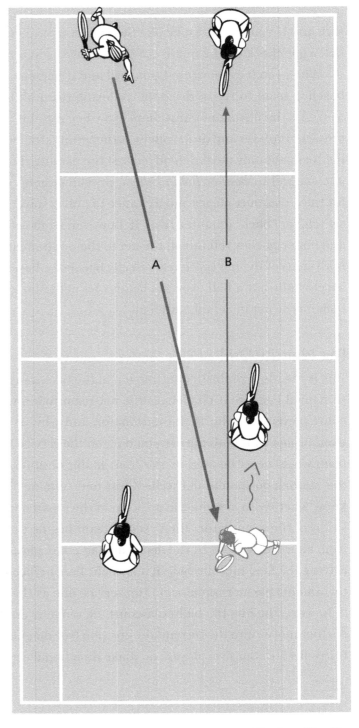

*The Art of Doubles*

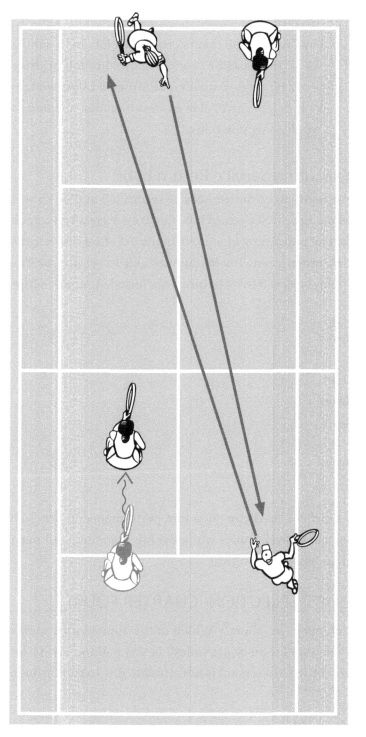

**Diagram 35**

## The Identity Drill: Scenario Two

In this identity drill, the deuce court player has chosen to hit a crosscourt volley, so he holds the crosscourt position while his partner moves to the terminator position.

immediately punished by the baseline team's crosscourt lob. In this most difficult version of the drill, the baseline team is allowed to lob or drive, and the net team may only hit angles, uglies, and drops on both volleys and overheads. To make it competitive, play to eleven points, needing to win by two, and then switch court positions.

## Covering and Executing Service Return Lobs

To evaluate a team's ability to cover the service return lob and to hone a team's ability to execute the service return lob effectively, I use scripts. Each player is given a piece of paper on which is written a list of service returns to be executed in the order given. The list applies *only* to service returns, and the rest of the point is played to its natural conclusion. A sample script might include:

1. Lob over net player
2. Hit crosscourt
3. Lob up the middle
4. Lob over net player
5. Hit down the line
6. Hit a dropshot
7. Lob over net player
8. Hit crosscourt

The scripts are an excellent predictor of actual performance in a match because the serving team never knows when the lob is coming and must react to the unpredictability of the return.

## INTELLIGENT SHOT SELECTION (CHAPTER FOUR)

Is my court position "deep" or "short"? Which of my opponents is closer to the net? Is this the time for an angle volley? Is this ball too low to hit down? Probably one-fourth of a second is not enough time to run through

*The Art of Doubles*

this litany, and therefore you must replicate different situations in your drills, and practice your responses to the given stimuli until they are absolutely automatic.

## Server's First Volley Placement

To avoid the server's first volley indecision, serve fifty balls to the deuce court and fifty balls to the ad court, all the while chanting to yourself "inside to inside" and "outside to outside" until you no longer have to think about it.

## Proper Targets for the Terminator's Volleys

The best way to integrate the Deep to Deep, Short to Short Axiom into your tennis game is to isolate particular situations that occur repeatedly in match play and practice making the proper decision to the point of absolute satiety.

The server's partner faces the first critical decision concerning the deep or short options, and this drill helps him practice those choices.

Three players are needed, but a fourth makes it more interesting. A server serves a ball to the deuce court, after which his job is finished. A receiver hits the service return directly *at* the server's partner, after which his job is finished. The server's partner must determine whether the ball speeding toward him is high enough to change its direction, and thus should be played to the target in the alley of the receiver's partner, or whether it is too low and should be played back toward the receiver, "short to deep" to keep his team out of trouble (see diagrams thirty-six and thirty-seven). If a fourth player is involved, he should assume the hot seat position of receiver's partner to practice digging out balls aimed in his direction. The rally is not played out beyond this point so that the server's partner may focus entirely on how he handles just one task. Be sure to give each player enough repetitions before rotating court positions. Changing places too soon can disrupt a learner's rhythm just as he may be about to master the technique.

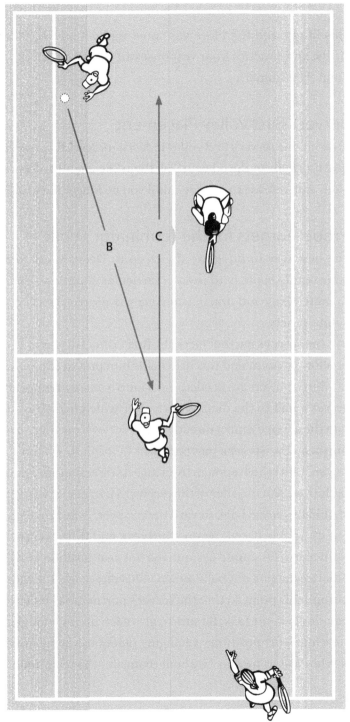

## Diagram 36
### Intelligent Shot Selection, Short-to-Deep Drill

In this drill, the server's partner is the worker. He knows that all balls will be hit at him. His task is to determine quickly the height of the ball aimed at him. His entire focus should be, "Can I hit down?" If no, the ball should be played "short to deep" to keep his team out of trouble. (See diagram 9.) If yes, the ball should be played "short to short" to end the point. (See diagram 9.) The entire exercise is designed to make the server's partner's judgment on ball height keener and thus his shot selection appropriate to the situation. This diagram shows the "short to deep" option for low returns.

*The Art of Doubles*

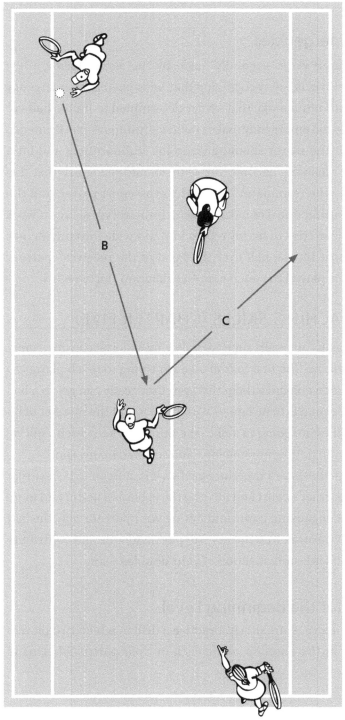

**Diagram 37**
## Intelligent Shot Selection

This shows the "short to short" option for high returns.

B

C

## Recognizing Emergencies

Another very common error, generally made by the server facing a low and wide service return, is not recognizing that he is having an emergency. Pride, hubris, or both often make that server determined to hit his half volley crosscourt when the emergency makes it virtually impossible. Prudence would indicate that the server should give up his stubbornness and lift a gentle lob over the receiver's partner. The team should recognize that this reverses their jobs—the terminator is now the crosscourt player, and the server is now the terminator. Try a drill in which the server serves a weak serve to a receiver who tries to hit his return low and wide into the server's alley. The server must lift the ball over the head of the receiver's partner, and then the point is played to conclusion (see diagram thirty-eight).

## SUPERIOR POACHING SKILLS (CHAPTER FIVE)

Superior poaching skills are really superior volleying skills laced with a great deal of guts and courage. The first task of a coach trying to teach players to poach successfully is to convince them that, yes, they really can get to a ball *way over there*. The second is to be honest with them about the number of humiliating mistakes they are going to make. The third is to keep each aspiring poacher's partner from huffily announcing, "You screwed up my shot."

If you are trying to become a superior poacher, it is difficult to believe that crossing into your partner's court and missing the volley is a better and more constructive idea than staying home and letting your partner play the ball. Ultimately, these sojourns across the net will pay dividends and contribute greatly to the health and sophistication of your doubles team.

## Poaching Drill for the Beginning Level

To build your confidence, start slowly. Practice a drill in which two players rally crosscourt from the baseline, while each of their partners begins in

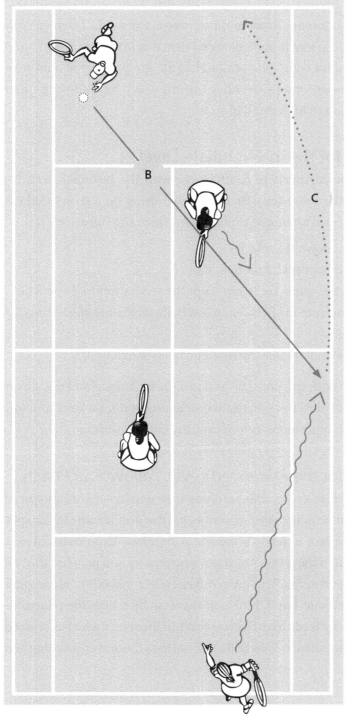

## Diagram 38
### Emergency Lob Drill

The reciever has hit such a sharp-ly angled return that the server will be unable to hit his half-volley crosscourt in this emer-gency. Thus she must execute a half-volley lob in a straight line over the head of the on-rushing reciever's partner.

the terminator position and tries to move across the net to intercept any ball struck from the *inside* (a right-handed deuce court player's backhand and a right-handed ad court player's forehand). The poacher should take care to use the correct target—the alley toward which he is moving—and avoid the temptation to hit behind himself.

## Poaching Drill for the Intermediate Level

After you and your partner feel comfortable with the beginner drill, try making things a little more realistic while still relying on a structured format. Orchestrate a drill among four players in which the rules are:

1. All serves are hit down the middle.
2. All service returns are hit back crosscourt.
3. The server's partner must try to intercept the service return. He will hit high balls and defer to his partner on low balls, retreating and letting them go through.
4. If the server's partner misses the shot, the point is replayed.

This exercise helps both the poacher practice his technique and the server practice crossing behind his partner when appropriate. Be sure to allow each player enough repetitions before rotating court positions.

## Poaching Drill for the Advanced Level: Follow Your Poach

This is an advanced poaching drill, and one that requires a fair amount of dexterity by the participants. The server begins the drill already in his split-stop, and his terminator is ready to poach. A "receiver" drop feeds an easy, high, poachable ball to the server's partner, who crosses and poaches the ball into the receiver's partner's alley. The receiver's partner should hold a spare ball in his non-dominant hand. If he can successfully return the poach, he does so. Otherwise, he feeds his ball crosscourt to the server who has crossed behind his poaching partner. This drill often catches the server standing and watching his partner rather than immediately crossing and filling in behind his partner. And it sometimes catches the poacher standing in the middle of the court watching his shot rather than following it, which, of course, leaves the team in an "I" formation.

When a team can execute all of these poaching drills confidently, it is then time for them to experiment with using signals and to decide whether they ultimately wish to become a signaling team or a freelancing team.

## JOBS ON THE COURT (CHAPTER SEVEN)

### Advanced Shadow Doubles Drill

This is the best doubles drill for crosscourt jobs. It can be played with two, three, or four participants, and it can be cooperative or not. It tests all skills needed to play good doubles with the exception of the overhead, and even that could be added in a more creative version (see diagram thirty-nine). The previous shadow doubles drill ended when the receiver played his first volley. In this more advanced version, the goal is as many volleys as possible, and each must be hit in the proper direction—inside to inside and outside to outside.

In Shadow Doubles for two players, all balls must be played crosscourt, and the player who misfires in this respect loses the point. One player serves to his partner, who makes a crosscourt return. Each player must complete a successful first volley after which he moves to his offensive court position. If the drill is cooperative, both players should hold an extra ball to be fed across the net immediately if an error is made. In this way, all points should contain a minimum of six or seven crosscourt volleys before the players are out of ammunition. Both players should make every effort to keep their volleys low and inside to inside, outside to outside. If the drill is to be uncooperative, well, then all bets are off. Each player looks for directional errors on the part of his practice partner and immediately makes him pay. If his

**Diagram 39**
## Advanded Shadow
## Doubles Drill

Shadow Doubles, so named because each player has a phantom partner, is the most important doubles drill a team can practice. So long as the ball is kept crosscourt, players can use it to hone point-ending skills; to be cooperative with one another and count the number of balls played across the net; to practice closing the net and executing sharply angled volleys; or to simply practice serving and gaining their net position from the base line. The possibilities are endless. All good doubles partners practice some form of this drill at least two to three hours per week. Servers and recievers always start the point. You could not do better than to practice starting it to your advantage—endlessly.

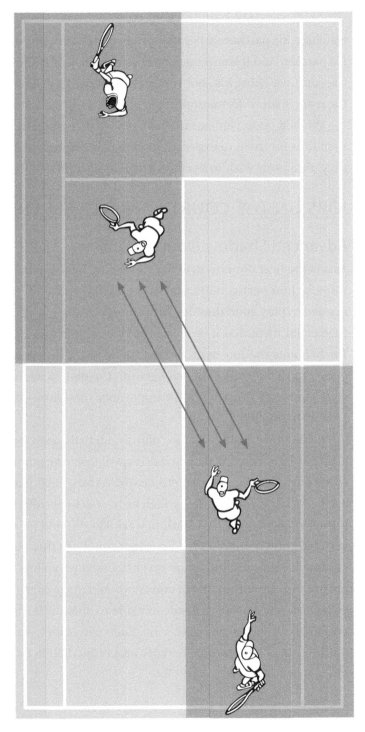

partner plays a ball outside to middle, he should immediately pay by losing the point with a sharp volley up the middle. Crosscourt lob volleys may be used against over-closers and drop volleys against laggards who hang back. Make sure that the receiver plays only the side he regularly plays in competition. Shadow doubles can be played for twenty years by a doubles team, and each would still learn something every time they took the court.

If three players are to be involved, the server and receiver play the non-cooperative version of the game, and the third player positions himself either as the server's partner or the receiver's partner, depending on which player's poaching skills needs the most work. Regardless of which job he assumes, his task is to try to enter the point and put the ball away in the direction of the proper target; thus he is exempt from the crosscourt rule.

If four players participate, each player should keep his job, that is, server, server's partner, receiver, or receiver's partner, for at least ten points. In this way, the receiving team can practice executing their responsibilities repeatedly, without having to change "hats" on each point. No lobs are permitted, and the point is played to its conclusion.

The basic structure of shadow doubles is the keystone for improving your expertise in every job you must execute on the court. It is well worth improvising versions for areas of weakness not covered above. Practice for long periods of time, but always quit before you get bored, tired, or sloppy.

## FLEXIBILITY (CHAPTER EIGHT)

## Practice Alternate Formations

Again, it cannot be overemphasized that you must practice the way you intend to play, and it is not enough to practice that way for just a few points. If your team is a bit shaky on how to use the Australian formation, play an entire match using it on every service point. If having to start a point from behind the baseline gives you an anxiety attack, play an entire match starting every point from that position. You do not need to use unusual formations in every match you play, but when the moment of necessity arrives, your flexibility must be smooth, confident, and practiced, not the last resort of a team unprepared for adversity. Don't forget to ask your friendly adversaries to use all of the unusual formations against you, too, and to use them often. There is no excuse for you, as a receiver, to panic if the opposition lines up against you in the Australian formation. Practice against it until you are as comfortable as you are hitting crosscourts.

## The Ping-Pong Drill

My students really appreciate this drill. It has no real value as far as actual doubles skills are concerned, but it helps communication, breaks up rigid thinking about "your side of the court" and "my side of the court," encourages players to be flexible, and it is fun.

All four players begin on the baseline. One ball is kept in play by all four, and each point is started with a drop feed. There is only one rule in the drill: No one player on either side of the net can hit two balls in a row. This means that when a player strikes a ball, his partner is responsible for the next, no matter where in the court it bounces. Players may choose to take the net or not, to use an "I" formation, or an automatic switch in court positions. Points are played to conclusion but immediately lost if a player on a team hits two balls in a row. Score is kept like ping-pong, with the winning team needing twenty-one points. An added benefit to the drill is that it aids racquet-watching skills because each player *knows* exactly which ball is his to play, no matter how far he must travel to reach it.

## COMMAND OF THE INTANGIBLES (CHAPTER ELEVEN) AND TIMING SPACE (CHAPTER SIX)

There is no drill that will allow you to practice taking more time to hit a ball other than your determination to increase it. Similarly, there is no magic-formula drill that will endow your doubles game with the perfect selection of depth, pace, or touch on every ball except the number of court hours you devote to the endeavor. There are, however, several drills that I have designed to improve students' racquet-watching skills, movement, anticipation, and hand-eye coordination.

## Peripheral Vision Drill

The best and simplest way to check or improve your peripheral vision and racquet-watching skills is to position yourself astride the center service line about halfway between the net and the horizontal service line. Ask your partner to stand behind the baseline opposite your position and feed you a ball, after which he is to move radically either to the left or right. You should be able to see the ball come off his strings and his lateral movement, after which you can volley competently into the open court. If you are initially unsuccessful, keep trying. Eye control does not take long to improve with a little diligence (see diagram forty).

## Experiment With Timing Space

Anticipation is a skill acquired over time, but to practice learning what happens when you take away an opponent's timing space, or what happens when you don't, try a simple crosscourt drill. Position yourself at the net in the crosscourt player's volleying position and have your partner begin crosscourt from you on the baseline. Ask him to hit any kind of shot he wishes, so long as he keeps it crosscourt. Within the rally, experiment with different depth volleys, and note the height of your partner's response to each of your volleys as it clears the net. In this way, you will begin to learn what is possible and impossible for a player in trouble or a player in no difficulty whatsoever. Count how many times his ball rises as it clears the net when you volley deep enough to remove his timing space, and note what happens when you don't. Make sure to use uglies to take away his timing

**Diagram 40**
## Peripheral Vision Drill

The net player is positioned in the center of the court—not a position normally assumed in doubles. He assumes this position in order to practice moving radically left or right. The practice partner on the opposite baseline feeds a ball and quickly moves left or right. This movement will occur before his ball actually crosses the net. In the time it takes for the ball to cross the net, the volleyer should be able to read not only the direction of the ball, but also the lateral movement of the player who has struck the ball if his eyes are glued to his opponent. This exercise teaches a player to watch an opponent's racquet, footwork, and body repositioning at the same time that he must watch a ball coming toward him. Four eyes would be better, but we only have two. Great doubles players make two do the work of four.

space. Practice angle volleys, drops, and angle overheads so that you hit nothing back to his waiting racquet.

## The Endless-Volley Drill

This drill has no net, but it helps players develop quick hands and good reflexes for volleys. One player positions himself at the "T," facing the fence. His partner stands about two feet from the fence facing his partner. Players are encouraged to hit rapid-fire volleys, and because there is no net, points are virtually endless. Students quickly find that they must bring their racquets to ready position at a lightning-like speed. They find that every ball comes back and that their ability to react to hard-hit balls improves dramatically. Again, making the drill more difficult than the match play engenders rapid improvement.

## Serve-at-Your-Partner Drill

This drill is not for the fainthearted, but it is effective. A player positions himself in terminator position either in the deuce or ad court while his partner serves first serves at him. The benefits for developing quicker hands at the net are obvious, but the drill can backfire if a player's volleying skills are not up to the drill. Some players may need to work into it slowly, starting back farther than the terminator position and asking their partners to begin by lobbing serves at them.

## CHARTING PROGRESS

The proof of your practice, of course, manifests itself in your match play record. I have included a charting sheet that I use to check my students' progress (see page 198). New computer technology can duplicate much of the information but not all of it. Computers cannot tell if the proximate cause of the point being lost is a judgment error or a positioning mistake or if the point was lost due to poor shot selection. Although these judgments are subjective, I feel they are better indicators of a team's overall progress toward mastery than the dry statistics produced by a machine. Someone with doubles expertise and knowledge of the doubles system you play—perhaps your coach—should do the charting.

Ultimately, there is no such thing as a useless drill, and no substitute for court hours. Use your imagination and devise drills that isolate the parts of your doubles game that make you feel insecure. And remember that it is a silly quirk of fate that the more you practice, the luckier you become.

---

## The Progress Chart

A check mark goes on whichever of these lines actually caused the point to be lost. **Note:** It is often interesting to count the number of points played in a set, and then count how many points ended in unforced errors. The results are sometimes shocking.

Date:     /     /
Player: _____
Player: _____

- ☐ First Serve (As a matter of interest, check here if missed.)
- ☐ Double Fault
- ☐ FHSR (Forehand Service Return)
- ☐ BHSR (Backhand Service Return)
- ☐ Error made by crosscourt player before middle of the point
- ☐ Error made by crosscourt player after middle of the point
- ☐ Error made by terminator.
- ☐ Lob
- ☐ Overhead
- ☐ Poach

*The Art of Doubles*

- ☐ Bad Judgment
- ☐ Poor Position
- ☐ Bad Shot Selection
- ☐ Good Placement (Check here if a point was won on a good placement.)
- ☐ Winner (Check here if service ace, service return winner, etc.)
- ☐ Opponent Forced Error (Check here if your player simply could not return opponent's great shot.)

## General Observations

- ☐ Did the team play with confidence?
- ☐ Were they too predictable?
- ☐ Did they visibly lose heart?
- ☐ Did they respond positively to the challenge of pressure?
- ☐ Were they flexible enough to use different formations when they needed them?

# 14

# Drills for the Highest Levels of Competition

······························

*Order and simplification are the first steps toward mastery of a subject—the actual enemy is the unknown.*

······························

*Thomas Mann*

The highest levels of competitive tennis demand excellence in every phase of execution. Drills must be designed to ensure that nothing is left to chance and that every eventuality, every situation that could arise in a match, is replicated in practice. Chapter thirteen focused on drills that refine shot selection and stroke production. This chapter deals with match-play situations. These drills train players to think clearly under pressure and are designed to produce smart, prepared, and confident doubles teams.

## MATCH AND CLOCK MANAGEMENT

In some parts of the country, both league and tournament matches are timed due to the scarcity of available courts. The usual time frame is two hours. If the match is tied at the end of two hours, a sudden death point decides the outcome.

The first and most important drill for teams competing under these regulations is to practice keeping the prematch warm-up to ten minutes or less. The rules allow for a ten-minute warm-up, but obviously if you can coax your opponents into completing it in seven or eight minutes, you have gained playing time. And if you are sloppy about it, or if you permit your opponents to meander around the court for fifteen minutes, you have lost valuable match time that might be important later. Practice completing the warm-up in five minutes. Then acquire the skill to encourage your opponents to begin the match early. For instance, at the end of five minutes offer, "Shall we take serves now?" Very often the reply is, "Sure." Of course, you cannot force your opponents to shorten the warm-up, but an honest attempt to lengthen the playing time from 110 minutes to 115 minutes is definitely worthwhile.

Unscrupulous opponents will sometimes employ stalling tactics when leading the match as time is running out. Use a role-playing drill to illustrate how to combat this tactic. A mock scenario might be:

A team has lost the first set and is trailing in the second set by 3-5. Their opponents are serving at 5-3 and are stalling on every point because there are only two minutes left on the match clock. What should the trailing team do?

Use another doubles team to act like "stallers," tying shoelaces, chatting unnecessarily, sauntering to pick up balls, and taking too much time between points. Ask them to play out the game as a bystander uses a stopwatch. Invariably, time runs out before the trailing team can figure out what to do. The answer is that they should consider losing that game as fast as they can, hitting balls into the net or out as quickly as possible. This strategy would give the trailing team the opportunity to serve, leading 5-4 with time still left on the clock. Since USTA rules state that the "match shall be conducted at the reasonable pace of the server," the serving team controls the tempo, and the stalling team can no longer employ those tactics. Of course, there is no guarantee that the serving team would hold and win the set, but it does give them a viable opportunity to reach the sudden death point if the match is tied at one set all.

Every team practice should include playing out sudden-death points. Serving teams decide whether they feel their best chance is to play Australian, use an automatic switch, or a freelance poach. Receiving teams decide who will receive the serve (it may be either player) and whether the return will go crosscourt or over the net man's head as a lob. All teams should practice both serving and receiving strategies. If you are unfortunate enough to have to perform under sudden death rules, you simply cannot expect to prevail without having a definite strategy in place for this gut wrencher of a match ending.

If you are fortunate enough to be allowed to play your matches with no clock restrictions, you still must manage the tempo and pace of the match, never allowing your opponents to dictate the pace at which the points are played. Again, use role-playing to illustrate this principle. Find a doubles team that really loves the chance to show its acting ability. One doubles team is told to play the set at a rhythm and tempo comfortable to them. The acting team is told either to stall or to hurry the match along at breakneck speed. The task for the first team is to learn methods of asserting themselves over opponents whose pace makes them uncomfortable. This is the basic principle of match management.

If you feel that the opposition is deliberately slowing down the match:

1. Never sit down on the changeover.
2. Run to pick up stray balls and return them to the server quickly.
3. Don't stop your feet; pace between points. It is calming.
4. Do more poaching; it ensures quick points.
5. Get your first serve in; it speeds up the match.
6. Never, never allow yourselves to become frustrated.

If you feel that the opposition is rushing you through the match:

1. Use the full ninety seconds on the changeover.
2. Walk to pick up balls and return them to the server only after you are ready to receive.

*The Art of Doubles*

3. Talk to your partner often; you have twenty seconds between points.

4. Hold up your hand if you are not ready to receive serve.

5. Do lots of offensive lobbing; it slows down the match.

6. Ignore the foot tapping across the net; have the poise to walk slowly.

## GROUNDHOG DAY DRILLS

As Dan Millman so eloquently put it, "A lesson will be repeated until learned." The Groundhog Day drills are based on that principle, inspired by the Bill Murray movie. Certainly the seventh game of a set is acknowledged as an important one, but other pivotal junctures in a set occur so often that they merit special practice and attention.

## 5-4

The dreaded 5-4 inspires prickly skin and stomach butterflies every time it is spoken aloud. How much better to hold serve confidently in this game than to succumb to 5-5 because your team was afraid to play aggressively. The 5-4 drill is very simple; the serving team practices that game until they prevail, but they must use a strategy that utilizes the terminator's ability to poach, fake, or cover a short lob on *every* point. It is too difficult for the server to feel that winning this all-important game is all on his shoulders. The more balls the terminator can intercept, the more likely it is that the team will hold serve. At this all-important moment in the match, the terminator is encouraged to take the risk of poaching on the outside serve to take the pressure off the server. The practice drill insists that the terminator must poach, fake, or cover the lob in each point—something he might be very reluctant to do under this much pressure. If he does not, the point is repeated. If the service game is lost, it is repeated until won, even if it takes the entire practice time. Make sure that the serving order is correct. The player who served first would be serving in this game. Of course, the corollary is being practiced at the same time. The receiving team should be instructed not to miss a service return, and to make it as difficult as possible for the serving team to hold.

## 2-5

So often when a team is serving at 2-5, the shoulders sag, and the racquets are dragging the ground. And yet the difference in the match is only *one* service break. The task in this drill is for the serving team to find ways to get the score to 5-5. If they do not succeed, even if they reach 4-5, the drill is repeated by starting at the beginning, 2-5. The goal is for the trailing team to learn to use straight-vanilla strategy:

1. First serve in.
2. Hit all server and receiver volleys crosscourt.
3. Be sure not to miss service returns.
4. Use no prideful or "hot-dog" shots.
5. Do not shrink from terminator duties.
6. Take your time; no hurrying to catch up.
7. Pay strict attention to court position.

The above points ensure you will be playing high-percentage tennis. There is a time for low-percentage tennis, but it is not at 2-5.

## 6-6

Not too many doubles teams actually enjoy playing tiebreaks. Most players immediately conjure up visions of sand slipping through an hourglass, and they tighten up dramatically. The drill for this malady is simple. One team is the "working" team, and the other is the "disrupting" team. They play a 12-point tiebreak (first to 7 by 2). If the "working" team loses more than two points in a row, the entire tiebreak is repeated from the beginning. The score could be 7-6, but they must start over until the "working" team manages to win the tiebreak without losing more than two consecutive points. So often a team will be down 0-3 in a tiebreak before they have even begun to settle in and breathe. This drill teaches players to concentrate from the first point forward, and because none of them relish having to start over repeatedly, they learn quickly.

## WHY DID YOU LOSE THAT GAME?

The answer to that question usually comes in various forms, none of them particularly constructive or helpful in righting the ship for the rest of the match:

1. I missed all of my returns.
2. All of my balls went out.
3. We suck.
4. I can't volley.
5. I need remedial help.

There isn't much in those subjective assessments that would enable a team to make on-court adjustments and improve their play in the next game. The cure for these pejorative evaluations is the proximate cause drill. Two doubles teams take the court and are asked to play one full game. At the conclusion of the game, the team that lost must identify *one point* which was responsible for the loss of the entire game. It is rarely a series of mistakes that loses a game for a team. It always comes down to one particular tactical error or untimely unforced error that causes a game to slip away. Some very common miscues that ultimately result in the loss of an entire game:

1. Missing your service return after your partner has missed his.
2. Failure to repeat an offensive lob after the first one was a clear winner.
3. Failure to execute a down-the-line return against an overeager poacher.
4. Crosscourt player incorrectly changing the direction of his volley.
5. More than one double fault in the game.

The key is to get teams to recognize that they didn't do *all* of these things in a game, but just one—and that one was enough. If you can turn all of that negative assessment into, "Yeah, if I had lobbed one extra time, we would have broken them. Next time I will," it keeps those nattering nabobs of negativity from spinning out of control. Often only small corrections are needed to turn an entire match around.

## THE MOMENTUM CHART

The momentum chart is a great tool. Two teams play four games using no-ad scoring (otherwise the chart takes too long to develop). As they are playing, an independent observer puts the appropriate dots either below the line or above it, depending on whether a team has won or lost the point (see diagram forty-one). When they have completed the four games, the observer connects all the dots. The sections should be mirror images of one another. Both teams can see where they were perhaps on a roll, winning six points in a row, and then suddenly lost the momentum by losing five points in a row. Often, a team will not even be aware that they had dropped five consecutive points. Teams should keep a momentum chart in their heads at *all times* during a match so that they are always aware of the ebb and flow of point distribution. The following is a list of momentum-grabbing opportunities in a match. Of course, each opposite would be a momentum-killer moment.

1.  A double fault to your partner—*don't miss the next service return!*
2.  A net cord to your team's benefit—*don't dump the ball in the net on the next point.*
3.  A long point that you win with a lucky shot—*don't follow it with a double fault.*
4.  Your opponent plays an out ball—*don't press your luck on the next shot.*
5.  You serve an ace—*make sure you get the serve in the box on the next point.*

Every match has peaks and valleys, but within that framework, you must learn to seize the day.

*The Art of Doubles*

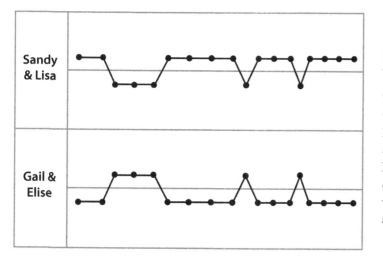

**Diagram 41**
**The Momentum Chart**

The momentum chart indicates the ebb and flow of the match. Points won are above the line and points lost are below the line. They will be mirror images of each other and will indicate which team has the momentum after four games.

## WHO ARE THOSE GUYS?

There are only four types of generic opponents—two back, one up and one back, "orange cones," and pairs in proper position at the net. There are two parts to the Who Are Those Guys? drill. In the first part of the drill, the working team assumes proper crosscourt and terminator volleying positions while the dummy team assumes one of the four generic formations. The task for the working team is to hit all balls fed to them to the correct targets against that particular formation. Targets that will defeat each formation are:

## Two Back
See diagram forty-two.
1. Angled volleys
2. Short angled overheads
3. Dropshot service returns—hit either straight or crosscourt
4. Drop volleys by the terminator

## One Up and One Back
See diagram forty-three.
1. Angled volleys

**Diagram 42**

## Targets Against a Baseline Team

When playing a defensive team properly positioned behind the baseline, hit only angles and drops. Avoid the middle of the court.

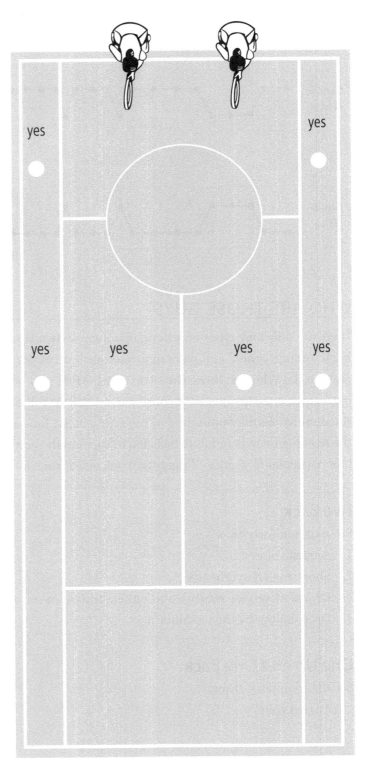

*The Art of Doubles*

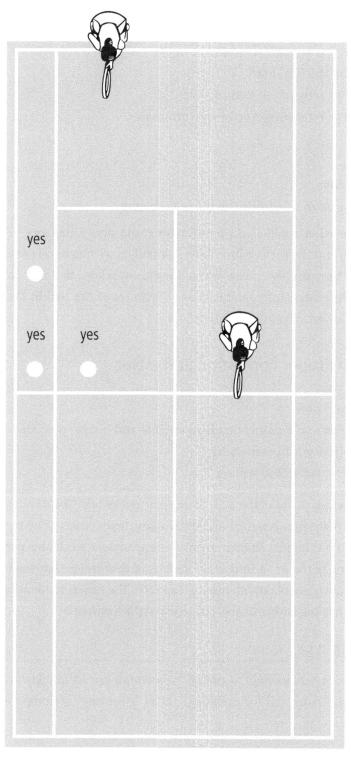

**Diagram 43**

## Targets Against a One Up, One Back Team

When playing a one up, one back team, hit drops, dropshots, and short angles in front of the back player. Short overheads should be directed at the up player.

2. Overheads hit at the "up" man

3. Dropshot service returns—hit crosscourt

4. Drop volleys hit *in a straight line* by the terminator

## Orange Cones

See diagram forty-four.

1. Play everything up the middle once the point begins.

(Orange cones are what I call two players who stand about halfway between the baseline and the service line. They normally have fast hands and good reflexes, but they simply do not move. They know whose ball it is on the outside, but they are totally confused as to who takes the ball in the middle because they are even on the court.)

## Good Teams in Proper Formation at the Net

See diagram forty-five.

1. Be deliberate and precise

2. Crosscourt player's volleys go outside to outside and inside to inside

3. Terminator volleys go short to short

4. You will pay for misdirected volleys

After the target-practice phase of the drill, teams play out points. The dummy team assumes one of the four generics, and the working team must utilize the correct targets for the situation. Dummy teams are encouraged to change personalities often. One of the most important lessons of this drill is that there are only four possible types of opponents you can face. The task is to identify which one you are dealing with and proceed to shred the formation.

## LOOKING FOR TELLS

In poker, a sudden eye movement, a twitch, or a cough are all quickly noticed by a pro and scrutinized for meaning. These "giveaway" actions are

*The Art of Doubles*

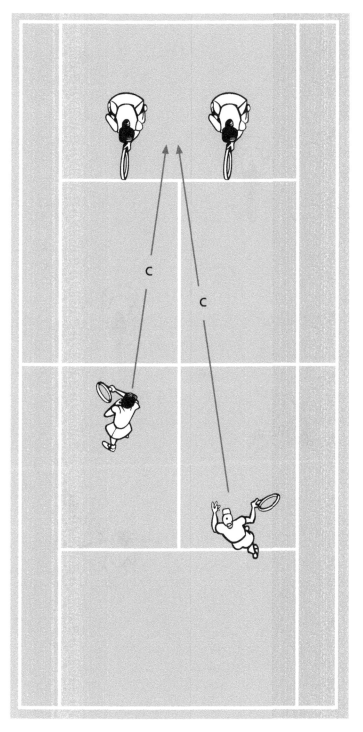

**Diagram 44**
## Targets Against Orange Cones

When playing against "orange cones," hit everything, everything, everything up the middle. They don't know whose ball it is.

## Diagram 45
### Targets Against a Properly Postioned Net-Rushing Team

When playing a good team in proper offensive position, follow the rules. Outside to outside, inside to inside for the crosscourt player. Short to short for the terminator if given the chance. Trying to get creative will lose you the point. Don't target the emergency half-volley lob.

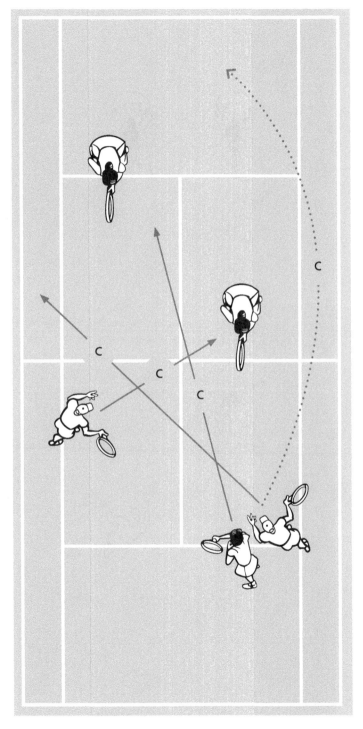

*The Art of Doubles*

called *tells*. And so it is in tennis. If you are very observant, you will notice many tells by the players across the net, and that shrewdness can be a big advantage for your team. Some very common tells:

1.  After a point is over, an opponent returns the ball to you by obviously rehearsing his forehand—a sure sign he has absolutely no confidence in it.
2.  Your opponents take their volleys in the warm-up, standing two inches from the net. Do they really know how to volley? Very doubtful.
3.  You ask for a lob in the warm-up, and the guy across the net cannot even get the ball to you. Will you be facing lob queens? No.
4.  One of your opponents screams, "I can't hit a service return to save my life," to himself. Excellent. He probably has talked himself into that one.
5.  Your opponents never talk. But this time, before serving to you, they do. Watch out. A rare poach is coming.
6.  You hit a perfect service return lob winner. Your opponents not only do not confer, but they also move to the next point without giving it a second thought. Think they figured out how to cover the next one?
7.  Ever warm up against a player who starts every rally with his backhand? That is a dead giveaway that he either hates his forehand or that it is very prone to "the yips"—that catatonic state where a player cannot remember how to hit the shot at all.

If you watch carefully, you may notice other tells in each match that you play. Be sure to share the information with your partner, and pounce on the weakness immediately.

There is really only one drill for tells, and that is to use a dummy team and have them explore the limits of their imaginations. Or you could have a coach mimic certain actions, and ask the watching players what each behavior indicates.

These drills are all relevant to actual situations that occur regularly in matches. The goal is to take the court as prepared as you can be for any eventuality or any behavior your opponents might exhibit. Whatever your predicament on the court may be at the time, in the highest levels of competition you can never afford to say that you haven't seen that before. The main objective of these drills is to produce teams that think well under pressure, that always have an answer to a problem, and that compete well even when not playing particularly well.

# INDEX

**A**

Ad court player, 10–11
  poaching by, 75
  in short court position, 51
Advanced shadow doubles drill,
  189–191
Alternate formations, practicing,
  191–192
Angle volleys, defending against, 95
Anticipation, components of, 138–143
Attitude, winning, 158
Australian serving formation, 86,
  119–121
  defending against, 123–124
Automatic switch, 86, 88

**B**

Backhand volley
  one-handed, 162
  two-handed, 62, 65
Balance
  checklist, 16
  drills for, 176–178
  emotional, 9–10
Ball direction and placement, 51
Ball-watching skills, 132–133
Baseline
  playing from, 43
  team, targets against, 206
Body language, 19–20
Bouncing, serve, 162

**C**

"California doubles" formation, 29, 85
Center ball, improper positioning on,
  36
Charting progress, 195–197
Check step, 141. *See also* Split-stop
Choking, 146–147
Clock management, 198–200
"Closing a match out," 157

Closing the net, 55, 57–58
  crosscourt player, 39
  hitting crosscourt and, 161
Coach, 15–16
*The Code* (USTA), 22
Communication, 17–27
  adverse circumstances and, 21–22
  body language, 19–20
  built on trust, 22
  checklist, 27
  drills for, 176–178
  off-court, 17–19
  on-court, as dialogue, 20
  rules of, 19–27
Confidence, 133
  drill to gain, 177
  flexibility and, 115–116
  as key to winning, 167
Controlling the net, 84–97
  checklist, 97
  drills for, 178–182
  other lobs and, 88–96
  proper formation at, targets against,
    208, 210
  relinquishing control, 43
  service return lob and, 85–88
Court assignments, 10–12
Court jobs
  checklist, 113
  drills for, 189–191
  focusing on your, 151
  receiver, 105–106
  receiver's partner, 107–113
  server, 99–103
  server's partner, 103–105
Court movement, rules of proper,
  140–143
Court officials, help from, 25–26
Court position, 28–44

checklist, 44
defensive, 40–44, 126–127
effect of variety in, 72–73
identity drill, 179–182
"nose on net," 48
offensive, 29–40
proper, 28–29, 44
take-away-the-net drill, 178–179
Court scenario, ball direction and
   placement, 51
Crosscourt lob, 29–30, 62
Crosscourt player, 29–31
  closing the net, 39
  communication and, 20–21
  dealing with lobbers, 92
  improper positioning on middle ball,
   36
  improper positioning on wide ball,
   34
  offensive positioning for, 32, 35
  outside to middle volley, 54
  receiving overhead smash, 42
Crosscourt shot, short-angled, 46
**D**
"Deep to deep," 47, 51
Deep to Deep, Short to Short Axiom,
  47, 49
"Deep to short," 47, 51, 109
Defensive lob, 46
Depth, 134
Deuce court player, 10
 in deep court position, 51
 poaching by, 75
 timing space of, 93
Diagrams, key to, 5
Doubles play, misguided statements
  about, 2
Doubles teams
  balanced, 6–16
  characteristics of successful, 4
  coach for, 15–16
  dream team, 6–10
  kinds of, 1–2
  lessons for, 168

nurturing character of, 12
  united front of, 23–25
"Down-the-line" service return, 79
"Down-the-middle" serve, 101
"Down-the-middle" service return, 80
Drills
  advanced shadow doubles, 189–191
  emergency lob, 187
  endless-volley, 195
  everything is good, 178
  for flexibility, 191–192
  identity, 179–182
  groundhog day, 201–203
  intangibles, 192–195
  for intelligent shot selection,
   182–186
  peripheral vision, 193–194
  ping-pong, 192
  poaching skills, 186–189
  for recognizing emergencies, 186
  serve-at-your-partner, 195
  server's first volley placement, 183
  for service return lobs, 182
  shadow doubles, 177
  take-away-the-net, 178–179
  targets for terminator's volleys, 183
  for tells, 211
Drop volley, 62, 137
Dropshot, 63
**E**
Emotional balance, 9–10, 176–178
Endless-volley drill, 195
Errors
  eliminating unforced, 117–118
  forced, 118
Ethical problems, overruling partner's
  call, 22
Everything is good drill, 178
**F**
"Fade and close" strategy, 95–96
Fear of losing, 147–150
Fear of winning, 147, 152–155
Finesse, 134, 137
5-4 drill, 201–202

Flexibility, 114–128
  Australian serving formation and, 119–121
  checklist, 128
  confidence and, 115–116
  defending against Australian formation, 123–124
  defending against monster serve, 125, 127
  drills for, 191–192
  eliminating unforced errors and, 117–118
  in face of lob queens, 127–128
  forced errors and, 118
  impenetrable opponents and, 127
  recognizing your predictable strokes, 119
  regaining your rhythm, 117–118
Floating ball, 57
Forehand, topspin, lefties and,10
Forehand volley, 162

**G**
"Go" poaching signal, 78, 80, 82
"Great hands," 142–143
Grip, continental vs. western, 151–152
Groundhog day drills, 201–203
Groundstrokes, topspin, 64

**H**
Half volley, 60–61, 103
High-percentage tennis, 46–47, 50
Hitter, 11
Hitting behind yourself, 56

**I**
"I" serving formation, 76, 121–123, 125
Identity drill, 179–182
Inside ball, 52, 53
"Inside to Inside, Outside to Outside" rule, dangers of breaking, 54
Intangibles
  anticipation, 138–143
  checklist, 144
  depth, 134–136
  drills, 192–195
  drop volley, 137

finesse, 134–136
  "great hands," 142–143
  pace, 134–136
  proper court movement, 140–143
  *sprezzatura*, 129–131
  sum of the parts, 143–144
  time, 131–134
  underspin volley, 137

**L**
League tennis, 170–173
  advantages of, 171
  drawbacks of, 172–173
  timed matches, 166
Lefties, topspin forehand, 10
"Linebacker eyes," 132
Lob
  deep, 48
  defensive, 46
  drill for emergency, 187
  service return. *See* Service return lob
  staggered formation, 85
  topspin, 65
  underspin, 64
  when to bounce, 91
Lob queens
  deep, ugly volleys against, 62
  flexibility in face of, 127–128
Lob volley, 62
Losing
  fear of, 147–150
  gracious, 128
  reasons for, 161–167, 203
Low-percentage tennis, 57, 59

**M**
Match management, 198–200
"Match tough," 157
Mental toughness, 145–159
  checklist, 159
  choking and, 146–147
  drills, 176–178
  fear of losing and fear of winning, 147–155
  play to win, 159
  practicing, 157–158

winning attitude, 158
the zone, 155–156
Mirror concept, 31–32
Momentum, 153
  loss of, 164
Momentum chart, 204–205
Monkey speak, 148–150

**N**

National Tennis Rating Program
  (NTRP), ratings, 171
Negative thinking, 148
Net, controlling. *See* Controlling the net
Net rushers
  deep, ugly volleys against, 62
  opponents, 37
"No CBS" rule, 52
"No percentage tennis," 52
"Nose-on-net" position, 47–48

**O**

One up and one back formation, 205, 207
Open tournaments, 175
Opponents
  concentrating on motions of, 139–140
  impenetrable, 127
  knowing preferred strokes of, 139
  net rushers, 37
  preconceived notions about, 165
  prematch fraternization, 23–25
  rushing through the match, 200–201
  slowing down the match, 200
  types of, 205
Orange cone formation, 208–209
Outside ball, 50, 52, 53
Overhead smash, 62–63
  defensive court position against, 42

**P**

Pace, 134
Partner
  ending partnership, 12–15
  overruling call of, 22
  receiver's, 107–113
  server's, 103–105
  shopping for, 9
  trusting your, 20

Performance anxiety, 147–148
Peripheral vision drill, 193–194
Ping-pong drill, 192
Placement, anticipation and, 138–139
Poaching the ball, 55. *See also* Poaching skills
Poaching skills, 67–83
  aborting poach, 71
  checklist, 83
  drill for, 186–189
  not following your poach, 74
  partner and, 76
  patience as, 70
  planning to poach, 68–71
  reasons to poach, 69
  server's job and, 77
  signals, 76–83
  strategies for poaching, 71–73
  targets and, 75
  when not to poach, 108, 110
  when to poach, 111
  where to hit poach, 73–76
Point
  beginning of, 45–46
  middle of, 47–50
Predictability, 119
Prematch warm-up, 198–199
Progress chart, 195–197
Punch volley, 134

**R**

Racquet speed, 134–137
Receiver, partner of, 107–113
Return. *See* Service return
Rhythm, regaining, 117–118
"Roundhouses," 163
Rushing, 131

**S**

"Second ball lobitis," 163
Serve
  bouncing, 162–163
  down the middle, 101
  flat, 65, 163
  holding, 99–100
  monster, defending against, 125, 127

returning successfully, 105–106
spin, 61, 163–164
wide, 102
Serve-at-your-partner drill, 195
Server, 99–103
  drill for first volley placement, 183
  nervous, 154
  partner's job, 103–105
  when partner poaches, 77
Service return
  "down-the-line," 79–80, 121
  offensive lob as, 48
  shifting position to meet, 140
Service return lob
  as approach shots to net, 63
  Australian formation, 86
  automatic switch, 86, 88
  covering, over partner's head, 90
  covering, up the middle, 89
  defending against intelligent, 95
  drill for, 182
  as high volley, 87
  for terminator, 85–86
Setter, 11
Shadow doubles drill, 177
"Short to deep," 47, 51, 184
"Short to short," 47, 51, 185
Shot placement, 138–139
Shot selection, 45–66
  bailing out of shot, 59–60
  beginning stage of point, 46–47
  checklist, 66
  closing the net, 55, 57
  drills for, 182–186
  high-percentage, 46–47, 50
  middle stage of point, 47–50
  poaching the ball, 55
  shots you don't need, 64–66
  shots you need, 60–66
  targets and, 50–52, 55
Shots you don't need
  big, flat serve, 65
  topspin groundstrokes, 64

topspin lob, 65
two-handed backhand, 65
underspin lob, 64
Shots you need
  dropshot, 63
  half volley, 60–61
  overhead smash, 62–63
  slice backhand, 63
  spin serve, 61
  volleys, 62
6-6 drill, 202–203
Slice backhand, 63
Smash, overhead, 62–63
Speed, racquet, 134–137
Spin serve, 61, 163–164
Split-step, 141. *See also* Split-stop
Split-stop, 100, 141
Sports psychology, 145
*Sprezzatura*, 129–131, 143
Staggered formation, 29–30, 85–88
"Stay" poaching signal, 79, 80, 82
"Straight vanilla" shot selection, 46,
  202
Swinging volley, 63
**T**
Take-away-the-net drill, 178–179
Targets
  against baseline team, 206
  against orange cone formation,
    208–209
  against proper formation at net, 208,
    210
  to defeat one up and one back for-
    mation, 205, 207
  to defeat two back formation, 205
  inside ball, 52
  opponents' alleys as, 73
  other, 52, 55
  outside ball, 50, 52
  for poaching, 75
  for terminator's volleys, 183
Tells
  drill for, 211

looking for, 208, 211–212
Tennis reputation, 22
Terminator, 29–31
  angle to ball, 37, 38
  closing the net, 58
  offensive position for, 32
  poaching, 74, 76
  service return lob for, 85–86
  "short to deep" play, 47
  using poaching signals, 79
Terminators, drills for volley targets,
  183
Time, mastering, 131–134
Timing space, 92–94, 178, 193, 195
Topspin, 61
  groundstrokes, 64
  lefties forehand, 10
  lob, 65
Tournament tennis, 174–175
Two back formation, target against,
  205
2-5 drill, 202
Two-handed backhand, 62, 65

**U**
Underspin lob, 64
Underspin volley, 137

**V**
Volley

angle, 95
backhand, one-handed, 162
drop, 137
first, 103
forehand, 162
punch, 134
two-handed, 162
types of, 62
ugly, 94
underspin, 137

**W**
Warm-up, prematch, 198–199
"Watcher," 28, 100, 106, 109, 115
Wide ball
  improper positioning on, 34
  offensive positions for, 32
  serving wide, 102
"Windshield wipers" theory, 33
Winning
  fear of, 147, 152–155
  three keys to, 167–169
Winning attitude, 158
Winning strategy, changing, 165–167
"Wonderer," 28, 100, 106, 109, 115

**Y**
"Yips," 163

**Z**
The zone, 155–156

*The Art of Doubles*